Between Sequence and *Sirventes*
Aspects of Parody in the Troubadour Lyric

THE EUROPEAN HUMANITIES RESEARCH CENTRE

UNIVERSITY OF OXFORD

The European Humanities Research Centre of the University of Oxford organizes a range of academic activities, including conferences and workshops, and publishes scholarly works under its own imprint, LEGENDA. Within Oxford, the EHRC bridges, at the research level, the main humanities faculties: Modern Languages, English, Modern History, Literae Humaniores, Music and Theology. The Centre stimulates interdisciplinary research collaboration throughout these subject areas and provides an Oxford base for advanced researchers in the humanities.

The Centre's publications programme focuses on making available the results of advanced research in medieval and modern languages and related interdisciplinary areas. An Editorial Board, whose members are drawn from across the British university system, covers the principal European languages. Titles include works on French, German, Italian, Portuguese, Russian and Spanish literature. In addition, the EHRC co-publishes with the Society for French Studies, the British Comparative Literature Association and the Modern Humanities Research Association. The Centre also publishes *Oxford German Studies* and *Film Studies*, and has launched a Special Lecture Series under the LEGENDA imprint.

Enquiries about the Centre's publishing activities should be addressed to:
Professor Malcolm Bowie, Director

Editorial Coordinator for French
Dr Nicola Luckhurst

Further information:
Kareni Bannister, Senior Publications Officer
European Humanities Research Centre
University of Oxford
47 Wellington Square, Oxford OX1 2JF
enquiries@ehrc.ox.ac.uk
www.ehrc.ox.ac.uk

LEGENDA

RESEARCH MONOGRAPHS IN FRENCH STUDIES

❖

Published in this series:

1. *Privileged Anonymity: The Writings of Madame de Lafayette*
by Anne Green
2. *Stéphane Mallarmé. Correspondance: compléments et suppléments*
edited by Lloyd James Austin, Bertrand Marchal and Nicola Luckhurst
3. *Critical Fictions: Nerval's 'Les Illuminés'*
by Meryl Tyers
4. *Towards a Cultural Philology:* Phèdre *and the Construction of 'Racine'*
by Amy Wygant
5. *George Sand and Autobiography*
by Janet Hiddleston
6. *Expressivism: The Vicissitudes of a Theory in the Writing of Proust and Barthes*
by Johnnie Gratton
7. *Memory and Survival: The French Cinema of Krzysztof Kieślowski*
by Emma Wilson
8. *Between Sequence and* Sirventes*: Aspects of Parody in the Troubadour Lyric*
by Catherine Léglu

LEGENDA

European Humanities Research Centre
Research Monographs in French Studies 8

Between Sequence and *Sirventes*
Aspects of Parody in the Troubadour Lyric

❖

Catherine Léglu

LEGENDA

European Humanities Research Centre
University of Oxford
Research Monographs in French Studies 8
2000

Published for the Society for French Studies by the
European Humanities Research Centre
of the University of Oxford
47 Wellington Square
Oxford OX1 2JF

LEGENDA is the publications imprint of the
European Humanities Research Centre

ISBN 1 900755 44 0

First published 2000

British Library Cataloguing in Publication Data
A CIP catalogue record for this book is available from the British Library

LEGENDA series designed by Cox Design Partnership, Witney, Oxon
Printed in Great Britain by
Information Press
Eynsham
Oxford OX8 1JJ

Chief Copy-Editor: Genevieve Hawkins

CONTENTS

ACKNOWLEDGEMENTS

This monograph is based on the second chapter of my doctoral thesis, 'The Voice of the Satirist in Medieval Occitan Poetry', which was submitted in 1995. Since then, a number of important new studies have appeared, all of which have altered the conclusions I had reached. My thanks to: Michael Moriarty, Michael Freeman, Linda Paterson, Sarah Kay, Ruth Harvey and my Ph.D. Supervisor, Simon Gaunt.

ABBREVIATIONS

❖

AH *Analecta Hymnica Medii Aevi*, ed. Clemens Blume and Guido Maria Dreves, 58 vols. (Leipzig: Riesland, 1911–78).

BS *Biographies des Troubadours: Textes provençaux des XIIIe et XIVe siècles*, ed. Jean Boutière and Alexandre H. Schutz, with Irénée-M. Cluzel (Paris: Nizet, 1964).

FEW *Französisches Etymologisches Wörterbuch*, ed. Walther von Wartburg, 24 vols. (Bonn: Schröder, 1925–83).

Frank István Frank, *Répertoire métrique de la poésie des troubadours*, 2 vols. (Paris: Champion, 1966).

NEB *The New English Bible* (Oxford and Cambridge: Collins, 1970).

PC *Bibliographie des Troubadours*, ed. Alfred Pillet, with Henry Carstens (Halle: Niemeyer, 1933).

PD *Petit Dictionnaire Provençal-Français*, ed. Emil Levy (5th edn. Heidelberg: Winter, 1973).

PSW *Provenzalisches Supplement-Wörterbuch, Berichtigungen und Ergänzungen zu Raynouards 'Lexique Roman'*, ed. Emil Levy, 8 vols. (Leipzig: Riesland, 1894–1924).

R *Lexique Roman, ou dictionnaire de la langue des troubadours comparée avec les autres langues d'Europe*, ed. M. Raynouard, 6 vols. (Paris: Silvestre, 1838–44).

Vulgate *Biblia Vulgata: Biblia Sacra iuxta Vulgatam Clementinam, nova editio*, ed. Alberto Colunga and Laurentio Turrado (Madrid: Biblioteca de Autores Cristianos, 1985).

INTRODUCTION

Parody marks the troubadour lyric from the outset. The earliest extant troubadour, Guilhem IX, composed a corpus of decorous love songs and bawdy pieces that appear to parody his own serious treatments of love.[1] As Pierre Bec has suggested in his anthology of burlesque poems, the significant corpus of satirical, parodic and burlesque songs extant in the troubadour lyric shows a playful subversion of the language of *fin'amors* that is both irreverent and crucial to its success: the *ars amoris* is followed by its parodic cure. However, some parodies may be more aggressive than others. The troubadour who composed the *coblas* found in *chansonniers JG* transforms selected stanzas from *cansos* by Bernart de Ventadorn, Peirol and Folquet de Marselha, rewriting them as scatological caricatures that seem to aim at more than simple amusement and may show the darker side of the process (Bec, 37, 38, 39). For example, Bernart's famous *canso* 'Can la frej' aura venta' opens with an image of fragrant dreams about his beloved:

> Can la frej' aura venta
> deves vostre pais
> vejaire m'es qu'eu senta
> un ven de paradis.
> (*PC* 70, 37, Appel, XXVII, vv. 1–4)

[When the cold breeze blows over from your country, it seems to me I feel a wind from Paradise.]

The anonymous author of the following *cobla* (*PC* 461, 202, Bec, 38) reproduces the metrical scheme and rhyme words but inserts a content that debases the image altogether:

> Quan lo petz del cul venta
> Dont Midonz caga e vis
> Vejaire m'es qu'eu senta
> Una pudor de pis.

[When the fart blows from the arse, from which My Lady shits and farts, it seems to me I smell a stench of piss.]

This *cobla* can only draw its comic effect when it is set beside its model; its parodic function rests in the dialogue between the decorous model, and what Bec terms the *contre-texte*. Laura Kendrick has proposed to read such texts as evidence of a ludic tradition and a poetics of play. In her monograph *The Game of Love*, such parodic debunking is viewed as a typical element of a poetry based on punning, double-entendres and aural games played by the written and performed texts.[2] Textual open-endedness of this sort subverts claims to consistent seriousness, suggesting a combative rejection of the ecclesiastical promotion of monologic discourse. Hence, the carnivalization of the lyric text produces infinite polyglossia, from a starting point that is, by inference, oral and irreverent.

This reading of the troubadour lyric only truly works if it is accepted that its secular authors were disaffected from clerical ideology. Simon Gaunt provides a more cautious reading of the irony in selected troubadour poetry which suggests that, far from being estranged from Latin learning, these poets founded their wordplay on sound rhetorical training.[3] Building on Linda Paterson's analysis of the rhetorical strategies deployed by individual troubadours, Gaunt's study of irony works from a basis of close textual readings that privilege the recognition of subtle textual 'signals to irony' which may have been invisible to less learned audiences. According to this theory, the knowledge and recognition of an élite culture (Latin or learned), far from being rejected, would have been essential to the success of ironizing rhetoric in songs.

Whatever the relationship may have been of the anonymous parodist cited above with the ecclesiastical authorities, it remains that his debunking of the 'vent de Paradis' is shockingly violent, and seems to rest on a relocation of the gaze (or nose) of the subject towards his *domna*'s lower body. The shift from an absent but directly addressed beloved to a disgusted description of a *Midonz* he goes on to call (in *J*) 'una velha merdolenta' [a shit-covered old woman] says less about his probable admiration for Bernart than about the aggression of misogyny when directed at the codes of *fin'amors*.[4] Yet the very banality of misogyny in the subtextual layers of the troubadour lyric makes such parodic attacks seem almost futile, a mere unveiling of a commonly held assumption. It could even show that the author of the *cobla* shares in the ecclesiastical perception of women, and strives to view *Midonz* as a sack of dung indeed.

If such ambiguity can be found in parodies of secular material, the question is all the more complex when dealing with parodies that touch on sacred texts. Tensions inherent in a parody of a troubadour *canso* are a matter of aesthetics and competing texts; the same cannot be said of a parody of liturgical material, where the ideology of at least one of the participating 'voices' plays a much more important role. Bec envisages the 'auto-négation' of a secular lyric text as homeopathic in effect: the song produces its own 'cure' for the ambiguities of its courtliness. Can the same be said for parodies of sacred texts? The multiple readings to be gleaned from songs signalling themselves as both clerical and jongleuresque are a source which deserves to be tapped more fully, when the clerical content touches on the sacred. In Bernart's song, the 'ven de Paradis' becomes an explicit reference to the sacred in the closing stanza and *tornada*. Bernart associates his *domna*'s praise of his songs with her enjoyment of divine favour, and hopes that 'tot'arma crestiana' will enjoy the joy he feels from her (v. 57). In the model text, it seems that the scent of Paradise is developed on semi-devotional lines.

Such imbrication of *fin'amors* and religious imagery is well attested. In his two studies of the phenomenon, Peter Dronke concludes that the realms of secular and spiritual song were permeable, and that the poetry of medieval Europe was both multilingual and multi-discursive. Certainly, the songs he cites to illustrate the theory show a pervading interpenetration of spiritual and erotic concepts, with exceptional irreverence in the poetry of Raimbaut d'Aurenga, who seems to play with inversed hierarchies between the carnal and spiritual worlds.[5] Raimbaut plays with the doxology, using it to support his plea to his lady, as if she were indeed his God, 'Deus, ajuda! *In Nomine Patris et Filii et Spiritus Sancti*! Aiso, que sera, domna?' (*PC* 389, 28) [God, help me! [...] So, what will it be, lady?]. This playful treatment of religious language is the work of a powerful nobleman, secure in his own unassailable social status, and does not pose a threat to ecclesiastical authority.

However open to further question such a reading of troubadour poetry may be, this study will not be concerned with the delicate dialogue between *fin'amors* and divine love. Instead, it will focus on a different issue related to parody, looking in particular at formal and textual relationships between troubadour songs from the earliest to the last generations, which share a metrical structure borrowed from the liturgical sequence or *prosa*. Most of these songs are classified under the generic label of *sirventes*: a song composed with the intention of moralizing, commenting on politics, satirizing a given situation or individual, or simply entertaining its audience.[6] A *sirventes* is also occasionally defined as a rewriting (*contrafactum*) of a previous song.[7] The systematization of *contrafactum* in the *sirventes* is associated essentially with Bertran de Born, who flourished in the later twelfth century, but occurs earlier, with mutual allusion signalled through the acknowledgement of borrowing: 'Lo vers comenssa/ A son veil, sen antic' [I begin the *vers* with an old tune and an ancient meaning] (Marcabru, *PC* 293, 32, XXXII, vv. 1–2). Thus the rewriting embedded in the *sirventes* may be equated with the rewriting inherent in parody.

Borrowed form and rewritten content invoke parody, especially in texts serving an epideictic function. The process of parody is neither simple nor linear, and plays on several layers of rewriting, involving recuperation and subversion. Such rewriting involves intertextuality, a subject that has played a key role in troubadour studies for nearly two decades. Jörn Gruber's *Die Dialektik des Trobar* presented a template for study of the dialogues between songs, but one which, as Maria Luisa Meneghetti has pointed out more recently, requires cautious use and careful definition.[8] Far from being a complex, codified dialectic, parody is a form of intertextuality that signals its terms of engagement more openly and directly than most others. Its very overtness and aggression make parodic writing seem marginal to the broad field of troubadour intertextuality. However, the twin concepts of the troubadours as participants in a formal and tropological network, and as skilled manipulators of vernacular *auctoritates* who cite and dispute with each other, are key elements in the parodic rewritings studied here.

Between the sacred sequence and the troubadour *sirventes*, there is a broad range of rewriting, recuperation and transgression that requires detailed attention. In the first chapter, I shall examine the evidence for clerical parody, as well as the theoretical approaches which can be adopted when dealing with parody of the sacred. This chapter will also consider the role of propaganda and politics in certain forms of intertextual appropriation. The second chapter will outline a specific corpus of songs in the troubadour lyric that share close intertextual connections, as well as a close link with the liturgical sequence. Chapter 3 will address issues of recognition and recollection of form in this respect, with reference to the role of both scribes and performers. Chapter 4 will present two forms of parodic rewriting, one aiming to recuperate, the other to destroy its models. Chapter 5 will explore the relationship of the versified sermon with parodic texts, negotiating the space between the *joglar* and the preacher.

This book will examine the interaction between the cleric singing in churches and cathedrals, and the *joglar* singing in the secular court. This is not to say that this constitutes the only 'origin' of troubadour lyric song. On the contrary, the Occitan lyric is a phenomenon produced by overlapping cultures, by travel and by moments of musical dialogue that have not always survived sufficiently clearly to be identified. Clerical and troubadour song have the advantage of both being inscribed in books, in which the finer points of influence can be traced. The connection between troubadours' songs and the 'clerical entertainment' of their peers deserves to be examined beyond the level of *contrafactum* or simple influence, since the same individuals sometimes heard, performed and occasionally composed these pieces of music, and their interaction, now divided by categories of academic discipline, was sometimes closer than might be supposed.

This book started out as one chapter of a doctoral thesis, and had no pretensions to be more than a micro-study of one instance of a parodic chain of songs, and how they might be related to a common metrical and discursive field. Expanding a chapter of 16,000 words to a study of this length has probably obscured its original intention. Hopefully, the present book will be received as a detailed exploration of one group of songs, chosen among a much wider body of texts; it aims to ask questions, rather than to present definitive answers to the problems produced by parodic rewriting and performance.

Notes to the Introduction

1. Pierre Bec, *Burlesque et obscénité chez les troubadours: Pour une approche du contre-texte médiéval* (Paris: Stock, 1984); see Don Monson, 'Parody, irony and burlesque', in *The Troubadours: An Introduction*, ed. Simon Gaunt and Sarah Kay (Cambridge: Cambridge University Press, 1999), 197–211.
2. Laura Kendrick, *The Game of Love: Troubadour Wordplay* (Berkeley: California University Press, 1988), 111; Bec, *Burlesque*, 173–5.
3. Simon Gaunt, *Troubadours and Irony* (Cambridge: Cambridge University Press, 1989); see also id.,'Marginal Men, Marcabru and orthodoxy: the early troubadours and adultery', *Medium Aevum* 59 (1990) 55–72; Richard Goddard, 'The Early Troubadours and the Latin Tradition' (Ph.D. thesis, Oxford, 1986); Jane Martindale, '"Cavaleria et Orgueill": Duke William IX of Aquitaine and

the Historian', in *The Ideals and Practice of Medieval Knighthood, II: Papers from the third Strawberry Hill Conference, 1986,* ed. Christopher Harper-Bill and Ruth Harvey (Woodbridge: Boydell, 1988), 87–116.

4. See Ruth E. Harvey, *The Troubadour Marcabru and Love* (London: Westfield College, 1989), 80–153.

5. Peter Dronke, *The Medieval Lyric* (London: Hutchinson University Library, 1968); id., *Medieval Latin Poetry and the Rise of European Love Lyric,* 2 vols. (2nd edn. Oxford: Oxford University Press, 1968), 98–111.

6. *PSW*, VII, 655; *R*, V, 238. See also *FEW*, XI, 534–5, *R*, XIX, 25–8; Joachim Storost, *Ursprung und Entwicklung des altprovenzalischen Sirventes bis auf Bertran de Born* (Halle: Niemeyer, 1931), 1–27; Suzanne Thiolier-Méjean, *Les Poésies satiriques et morales des troubadours du XIIe à la fin du XIIIe siècle* (Paris: Nizet, 1978), 26–32; Dietmar Rieger, *Gattungen und Gattungsbezeichnungen der Trobadorlyrik* (Tübingen: Niemeyer, 1976), 68–119.

7. Frank M. Chambers, 'Imitation of form in the Old Provençal lyric', *Romance Philology* 6 (1952–3), 104–20.

8. Jörn Gruber, *Die Dialektik des Trobar: Untersuchungen zur Struktur und Entwicklung des occitanischen und französischen Minnesangs des 12. Jahrhunderts* (Tübingen: Niemeyer, 1983); Maria Luisa Meneghetti, 'Intertextuality and dialogism in the troubadours', in *The Troubadours,* ed. Gaunt and Kay, 181–96.

CHAPTER 1

❖

Parodic Sequences and Peire Cardenal

In a scurrilous song attacking *clergues*, the troubadour Peire Cardenal criticizes their disruption of the office of Matins and specifically of its liturgical chant:

> E en loc de matinas an us ordes trobatz
> Que jazon ab putanas tro.l solelhs es levatz,
> Enans canton baladas e prozels trasgitatz.
> (*PC* 335, 64, Lavaud, XXXIV, vv. 19–21)

[And in place of Matins, they have composed an order [of service]: that they should lie with whores until the sun has risen, and sing *baladas* and travestied *prosae* instead.]

A *prosa* or *prosula*, 'small prose', is a form of trope inserted into the liturgy of the Mass, in addition to the existing chant. Connections between these forms of sacred chant and troubadour melodies have long been attested. The corpus of hymns and para-liturgical material found in the manuscripts housed in Saint-Martial-de-Limoges was disseminated over the Occitan and Northern Spanish regions, and shares some melodies with troubadour songs.[1] When Peire Cardenal speaks of monks, friars or clerks singing *prosae* they have twisted or altered, the reference may be to a tradition in which he, a former canon, may have been trained. Peire Cardenal's *vida* states that he was born into a noble family of the town of Le Puy-en-Vélay and became a canon at an early age. He trained to become a cleric, but fell into the secular life instead (*BS*, L):

E cant era petitz, sos paires lo mes per quanorgue en la quanorgia major del Puei; et apres letras, e saup ben lezer e chantar. E quant fo vengutz en etat d'ome, el s'azautet de la vanetat d'aquest mon, quar el se sentit gais e bels e joves. E molt trobet de bellas razos e de bels chanz.

[And when he was little, his father placed him in the greater canonry of Le Puy, to become a canon; and he learned letters, and knew how to read and sing well. And when he came to manhood, he acquired a taste for the vanity of this world, for he felt himself to be joyful, handsome and young. And he composed many good *razos* and good songs.]

Peire Cardenal is presented as a cathedral canon, trained in the cathedral school of Le Puy-en-Vélay, who later turned away from his spiritual training, and used his knowledge of music and letters to compose secular songs, especially *sirventes*. His devotional song to the Virgin, 'Vera vergena Maria' (*PC* 335, 70, XXXVIII), was linked by Lavaud to the 'Salve Regina', composed in Le Puy in the eleventh century. Despite his continued use of elements of his original training, Peire Cardenal's surviving corpus of songs is satirical, and markedly anti-clerical.

Peire Cardenal's career path is not unusual. The troubadour *vidas* are of debatable historical value, but indicate the expectations of readers and scribes about the social origins of poets. The troubadour Gausbert de Poicibot is said to have been an oblate in the monastery of Saint-Léonard-des-Chaumes, led into the secular life by his desire for women (*BS*, XXIX). Uc de Saint-Circ's *vida* states that he was sent to study in Montpellier by his brothers, but spent his time studying the poems and lives of the troubadours and eventually left to become a *joglar* (*BS*, XXXIII). The canon Daude de Pradas, on the other hand, remained in regular orders (*BS*, XXX), as did the Monk of Montaudon (*BS*, XLVI). In the twelfth century, the troubadour Arnaut Daniel is said to have left off his learning in order to become a poet (*BS*, IX). Giraut de Bornelh is said to have spent his summers touring as a troubadour, accompanied by two *joglars*, and his winters studying in *escola* (*BS*, VIII). He was reluctant to marry and donated all his wealth to his relatives and his local church (VIII, 6). His contemporary Arnaut de Marueil was a clerk of low birth who found it impossible to earn a living from his learning, so turned to a peripatetic career (*BS*, VII).[2]

Peire travelled around courts with a *joglar* who performed his songs, and seems to have preserved his texts in written form. The *vida* is signed by a scribe, Miquel de la Tor, who states that he compiled a collection of Peire's texts in the city of Nîmes around the time of the death of the poet, who lived to be nearly 100. This anthology has not survived, and was probably related to another lost manuscript, a collection of troubadour songs compiled by Miquel de la Tor in

Montpellier around 1300.[3] While this indicates that Peire was less careful with the transmission of his songs than his near-contemporary Guiraut Riquier, who left a collection of songs complete with their date of composition and notes on performance, it also suggests a poet who used his book learning to create an accessible archive of songs.

According to Peire Cardenal, the monks he attacks are performing *prosae* they have altered in some way. The term *trasgitatz*, the past participle of *trasgitar*, may be translated in a variety of ways. Levy and Raynouard suggest 'bateler, jongler, barioler', 'travestir' or 'entremêler'.[4] The clerks described in this song are the composers and performers of songs that may, according to the range of possible definitions available, be burlesqued or merely entertaining; the sense of 'entremêler' is seductive, in its connotations of generic admixture. 'Bateler, jongler' also imply an idea of travesty and of jongleuresque public performance.

What evidence there is of vernacular *prozels trasgitatz* that may have been sung by monks is slight. One possible example may be the anonymous song 'Ara lausatz', which expresses the bawdy desires of a monastic community through a parodic song of praise:

Ara lausatz, lausat, lausat
Li comandament l'abat.
Bela, si vos eravatz
Monja de nostra maison,
A profiech de totz los monges
Vos prendriatz liurason.
Mas vos non estaretz, Bela,
Si totzjorns enversa non
  Ço ditz l'abat.

[Now sing praises! Praised, praised be the commandment of the abbot. Lovely girl, were you a nun in our house, you would receive tribute to the benefit of all the monks. You will not spend a day there, lovely girl, unless you are on your back. So says the abbot.]

Peter Linehan's account of the riotous disturbances at the Dominican convent of Las Dueñas in Zamora in the year 1279 provides ample evidence of the uses to which liturgical and secular song could be put. The nuns attacked their prioress by singing and composing 'cantilenas malas et turpas' against her, while others chanted insults. The *Te Deum* was sung in the chapel to signal triumphant rebellion, and, on one occasion, a group of nuns who had taken friars as lovers seem to have enacted a parody of a liturgical ritual: '[W]hen the friars had gone away, they processed solemnly through the cloister, attributing the names of friars to each other and singing a chant as though they were accompanying a corpse to its grave.'[5]

Such parodic treatments of liturgical material have been inferred rather than identified in the relationship between the tropes and *versus* of the Aquitainian corpus and the troubadour *vers*, which were initially composed in the Limousin dialect. In his study *L'Ecole musicale de Saint Martial-de-Limoges*, Jacques Chailley established an etymological connection between Latin para-liturgical *versus* and Occitan *vers* which has proved enduring. The corpus of tropes, *prosae* and *versus* collected in the abbey of Saint-Martial-de-Limoges probably gives an accurate sample of music as it was produced and experienced in Aquitainian monasteries. James Grier has noted that there is only circumstantial evidence for their exclusively monastic origin, but that the *versus* corpus in particular suggests that around 1100, a number of regular clergy who had sophisticated tastes in music, Latin poetry and questions of doctrine began to produce songs destined for 'less formal, but still sacred, occasions'.[6] According to Grier, the manuscripts that made their way to the library of Saint-Martial-de-Limoges were probably produced in other major abbeys, or houses assocated with them; he cites Saint-Léonard-de-Noblat, Saint-Yrieix and Aurillac, as well as religious houses in Toulouse. However, there is evidence that the trope corpus was sung outside the immediate confines of the cloister. For example, the chronicler and composer Adémar de Chabannes notes that the cathedral canons of Saint-Etienne and the monks of Saint-Martial-de-Limoges would perform tropes and lauds together on occasion.[7]

Outside the field of formal and metrical borrowing, which has been the most studied aspect of the question, little has come to light that may prove a direct connection between the composers of Latin *prosae* and of vernacular *vers*. One outstanding exception does exist, in the form of the thirteenth-century troubadour Peire de Corbiac (Courbian).[8] Peire de Courbian's only surviving troubadour song is a devotional *canso* to the Virgin (*PC* 338, 1); he also left a long text, *Lo Thezaur*, in which, in addition to a demonstration of doctrine, he lists the material he knows from the *trivium*, *quadrivium* and a selection of vernacular romances and histories. At the end of this extended display of expertise, Peire de Courbian turns his attention to singing:

Senhors, encar sai ieu molt be vezadamens
Chantar en sancta glieiza per ponhs e per accens,
Triplar Sanctus et Agnus e contraponchamens,
Entonar seculorum que nol faill us amens,
E far douz chantz et orgues e contrapointamens,
E sai be mo mestier aperceubudamens,
Tot caresme carnal, quatre temps et avens.
Eu sai be cansonetas e vers bos e valens,
Pastorelas apres amorozas, plazens,
Retroenchas et dansas, gent e cortesamens.
(vv. 496–505)

[My lords, I also know well how to sing visibly [from sight?] in holy church with *punctum* and *accentum*, to do a *triplum* of *sanctus et agnus*, to intone the *seculorum* contrapuntally so that the Amen won't be missing, and to do sweet singing, *organum* and *contra-punctamentum*; and I know my craft very obviously: all Lent, the four seasons and Advent. And I know well [how to perform] little *cansos* and good and worthy *vers*, learned, loving and pleasing *pastorelas*, *retroenchas* and *dansas* nobly and in courtly style.]

Organum is early polyphony, as opposed to *contrapunctamentum*, its sophisticated development. The *punctum* is the simplest neume form of a dot or dash and *accentus* is the simplest form of chant. *Triplum* is the third voice-part of a motet, above the *duplum*, the voice above the tenor, the lowest part of the motet. Peire is boasting of a sophisticated set of musical skills for a clerk active *c.*1230–50, with evident experience of the northern French motet corpus.[9]

This section of the *Thezaur* makes an explicit link between the form of church singing practised by this learned clerk, and the performance of light vernacular material. This is consistent with the skills attributed to cathedral canons, whose festivals in cities such as Besançon could include the performance of *chorae* in the choir at Easter, with the inclusion of *rondeaux* and *virelais*. The intermingling of secular dance and liturgy was widespread,[10] and might not have been restricted to specific festivals. In 1404, the vicar general of Narbonne complained that the priests sang in the style of a *virelai*, 'with light voices and modulations', at the elevation of the Host.[11] The close connection between church and secular singing is made explicit by Guerau de Cabrera who informs the *joglar* Cabra that he cannot 'upar/ ni organar/ in glieiza o dedinz maizon' [whoop or sing *organum* in church or in a house] (*PC* 242a, 1, Pirot, 1, vv. 211–13).

The Aquitainian corpus of songs is overwhelmingly spiritual, with a few topical and secular exceptions. In the absence of more ample evidence of interpenetration, it would be useful to examine the ample corpus of Latin liturgical parody.[12] There is a large and varied corpus of Latin liturgical parody, studied in detail by Paul Lehmann and, more recently, by Martha Bayless. These texts are disruptions of the specific words of liturgical ritual and chant, and as such have been the focus of some scrutiny, in terms of the degree of subversion this process may imply. These texts are embedded in traditions of performed liturgy that suggest an ambiguous culture; the cathedral canons at Sens, for example, are said to have performed a complex dance in which they threw a ball to one another according to a set pattern while singing the *prosa* 'Victimae paschali laudes'.[13] These are *Prozels trasgitatz* indeed, but of an ambiguous sort, since they appear to be received as serious devotional practice.

The Mass, when performed in its set form and context and by appropriate persons, is an act constitutive of community, binding in its ideological connotations, and essentially unalterable in form, except with respect to the liturgical calendar. According to Sanda Golopentia-Eretescu, parodic Masses are inherently subversive: 'Le parodieur est un réducteur, un agent essentiellement négateur, tout comme le bouffon, le clown, le sot des sotties, le libelliste, le pamphlétaire, le caricaturiste.'[14] To reduce and to negate is to deny the dignity of a given model, even to debase it. Golopentia-Eretescu, who deals specifically with the activity of clowns, reads parodic Masses as 'une pratique réductrice ludique', in opposition to the serious action of performing the Mass in church.

However, the activities of clowns and jesters are dependent on the approval of those in authority, and tend to articulate a conservative agenda. The parodic masses and sermons of the Middle Ages have more often been perceived as ludic performances, which had their own set place and order within the liturgical year, performed at Christmas and Easter by designated individuals. This implies a ritualization of the parodic Mass, which becomes an established element of the liturgical calendar, and does not, as a result, pose any perceptible threat. Jacques Heers prefers to interpret parodic offices as an insiders' game, 'des divertissements d'initiés' which might have aimed to shock, but did not imply any subversive intent.[15]

Some recent studies of parody have indeed suggested that formal parody need not depend on critical readings of its model.[16] According to Linda Hutcheon, the definition of the Greek term *parôdia*, 'para-ode', as a 'counter-song', ignores the other sense of the prefix *para-* as 'beside' or 'alternative'. A *para*-song is therefore both a riposte and an addition to the model song, engaged in a paradoxical relationship which she theorizes as repetition with critical difference. For Hutcheon, 'Parody [...] is a form of imitation, but imitation characterized by ironic inversion, not always at the expense of the parodied text'. It is 'repetition with critical distance, which marks difference rather than similarity'.[17]

Parodic effect depends on context. Peire Cardenal's famous attack on the clergy, 'Tartarassa ni voutor' (*PC* 335, 55, LXXIV), is a parody of Bernart de Ventadorn's lovely and wholly unrelated *canso* 'Era.m cosselhatz, senhor' (*PC* 70, 6). Peire's song is one of the most famous texts produced in the aftermath of the Albigensian crusade, comparing clerks and preachers to buzzards and vultures circling over the putrefying flesh of a dying man, ready to take his wealth (vv. 1–8). The song condemns the activities of the French and of clerics (vv. 15–16); turning into a sermon, it exhorts the listener to abstain from rebelling against God, and to repent (vv. 25–40). The text probably did not circulate in secret, since it subsists in four manuscripts, *IKCR*, two of which were produced in Languedoc. In this song, the aesthetic effect of the invective would have been enhanced by prior knowledge of Bernart's *canso*, playing on the audience's sentimental associations with the melody.

An analogous song by Peire Cardenal, 'Clergue si fan pastor' (*PC* 335, 31, XXIX), seems to provoke a different form of parodic reading. The song is transmitted in eleven manuscripts, and is a *contrafactum* of a *canso* by Peire Vidal. The song also appears in an inquisition register recording a trial held in 1324, as evidence of the anti-clerical opinions of a group of noblemen in the Pyrenees.[18] A witness to the activities of the accused twenty years earlier states that he saw a knight recite the first *cobla* of this song in church, as he watched his brother, a bishop, celebrate Mass. In this trial it is the intention of the individuals who chose to learn and pass on the words of the song that matters, not those of the original author. It seems that context is essential to the song's effect; the performer of the *cobla* intends it as a comment on the behaviour of a bishop, and chooses to recite it during Mass, thereby subverting the sacred ritual as it is being enacted.

A survey of recent work on parodic texts shows a recurrent attempt to reinscribe parodic activity as a subversive gesture. Kathryn Gravdal has used Hutcheon's theory of parody to point out that parodic texts exemplify a form of intertextual aggression: the model text is repeated with a difference in the content that expresses criticism.[19] This is definitely the assumption made by Gormonda de Montpeslier, a *trobairitz* who wrote a corrective parody of Guilhem Figueira's *sirventes* against Rome (*PC* 217, 2).[20] Guilhem's *sirventes*, which is twenty-three stanzas long, is itself a parody of a lengthy devotional song to the Virgin, 'Flors de Paradis' (*PC* 461, 123). He states that he has chosen to use a melody he likes (v. 1), but the song is more than a simple *contrafactum*. The Marian song opens several *coblas* with the address 'Verges', building on standard epithets to the Virgin. Many of the *coblas* of Guilhem's *sirventes* open with an address to a feminine Rome, an allegorical figure he calls 'enganairitz' [deceiver] (v. 15). In turn, Gormonda effects a systematic rewriting of the *sirventes*, without reference to 'Flors de Paradis' (*PC* 177, 1). According to her twenty-stanza-long text, Rome has been besmirched by the attack of this 'avols hom' (v. 46). She works through each of Guilhem's accusations and refutes them, in what Katharina Städtler has interpreted as a staged disputation.[21] Städtler proposes that these songs were produced in the midst of intense political and theological conflict, between 1226 and the early months of 1229. Guilhem Figueira is not a Cathar, and Gormonda's text is not explicitly the product of anything other than a pro-crusade political position. Support for Rome is equated with correct ideology and pro-French opinion, in a partisan exchange. The devotional model, 'Flors de Paradis', may of course be another propagandist text, but it has not been dated. Beyond this cycle of text and para-texts, it seems that Guilhem Figueira's parody retains its subversive potential. In 1274, a bourgeois of Toulouse admitted to an inquisitor that while he did not possess a book containing the song, he had heard it performed, and could recite the first *cobla* from memory.[22] Circulating in written and memorized form, the song clearly had connotations of political dissent.

Texts produced during the Albigensian crusade are not simply ludic subversions of the sacred; they are embedded in a context in which the clergy and the church of Rome did not enjoy an unassailable position. Vernacular texts circulating in the laity's memories and libraries are potential instruments of political comment. By contrast, Martha Bayless's work on Latin sacred parody leads her to conclude that its ultimate purpose is a reassertion of its status via a celebration of its familiarity.[23] In this formulation, parody may reinforce as well as criticize the textual model it inevitably perpetuates.[24] A reader of a parody may even come to learn the structure and content of the model without needing to refer to it.[25] In the texts cited above, however, it seems that familiarity is the easiest vehicle for the expression of contempt.

Parody tends, as a result of such examples as this, to be merged with definitions of satire, a process which may be misleading. In his influential edition of Latin parodies, Paul Lehmann distinguishes between ludic texts which amount to word-play, and those which present political or social comment. He reserves the term 'satirical parody' for personal attacks alone.[26] This does not seem completely satisfactory, since his definitions do not resolve the problem of the political dimension that may be read into negative depictions of an institution. Bayless attempts to solve this problem by positing a satirical parodic genre, which she calls 'social parody'.[27] Social parody addresses failures in the function or ethics of a given institution, without seeking to attack its status or powers; the clergy may be criticized for drunkenness, but their right to be clergy is not questioned.

This 'social' reading only works part of the way, however, since the Mass and the Bible, though undeniably used in order to constitute a social and ideological community, are primarily texts which address society tangentially, through the community constituted by the act of performing the Mass itself. Performers may attack and distort the words of the liturgy, but they do not attack the doctrines of belief, nor the notion of a Christian community *per se*. Furthermore, to suppose 'social comment' to be the primary purpose of such distorting re-writings is to assume that a specific group is being criticized.

Hutcheon's evaluation of the problem, in this context, is more useful. She proposes a reading of parody and satire as instances of specific usage of the rhetorical trope of irony. Parody functions 'intra-murally' on a textual level, superimposing texts in order to bring out ironic reflections and reinterpretations of statements or precepts. Satire, meanwhile, functions 'extra-murally': the text causes the reader to engage in a pragmatic evaluation of the social and political referents surrounding and producing it. Both parody and satire function through a process Hutcheon calls 'transcontextualization': the form and content of a given text or ritual are removed from their appropriate frame, and reset in another in order to throw new light upon it. Satire in parodic texts, therefore, addresses a context outside the dialogue between model and parody, and irony is used to judge its object, rather than play with a double-voiced text.[28] Gérard Genette notes an analogous relationship between irony and parody in his use of the term 'littérature au second degré', a term referring to juxtaposed or double-voiced texts and, in colloquial speech, to ironic, 'double-edged' remarks.[29] A satirical parody would involve a double-voiced text which also causes the reader or spectator to reconsider his or her attitude towards a given social or political object. From a double-voiced text to a triple-voiced text (one voice addressing the 'extra-textual' world) is a complex journey, and one which, inevitably, will be contested by individual receptors.

This approach, while useful, has several drawbacks. In assuming that satire is a genre, it ignores the fact that satirical writing is definable not as a formal device, but primarily as a discursive strategy of attack, which may be articulated within the formal or textual field of parody. The interaction that takes place is in fact between a discursive strategy (satire), a formal device (parody) and a rhetorical trope (irony), which work together to produce a parodic text with satirical effect.[30]

Hutcheon's theory also seems to overestimate the 'extra-mural' references which may be made by satirical strategies. In the troubadour lyric in particular, attacks on society in twelfth-century songs are probably to be read less as mimetic discussions of social issues than as a text-based polemic using a constellation of fictional types. For example, Marcabru's songs have been read as a satirical attack on *fin'amors* poets' claims to idealism as a cloak for debauchery. The likelihood of their reflecting contemporary concerns with the mores of castle-dwelling households is debatable.[31] To assume that such texts are essentially mimetic is to fall in with the rhetorical game; the 'agent essentiellement réducteur' constructed by the clown or pamphleteer seems to acquire a power not confined to rhetoric.

This raises a significant problem. Parody of liturgical material may be received as a reinforcement of the authority possessed in the model: the Mass or its chants are not undermined, but used for their familiarity to construct comic or hostile representations of the clergy. The import of these depictions is difficult to assess, given their level of satirical intent (which may lie in the hands of audiences and performers alone). They may either present a threat to the established order, or be its best allies. Given Peire Cardenal's own clerical training and his extra-mural anti-clerical agenda, we see a complex process in action, in which the parodic activity within the cloister may be reinscribed as a subversive device, in the eyes of an author who is himself writing a work of sacred parody.

Peire Cardenal's attack on *prozels trasgitatz* comes in the middle of a poem that opens as a Credo and turns into a satirical, increasingly obscene attack on a group of monks involved in catechetical preaching in this period. Again, Peire's text is the product of a tense and conflictual context, in which the clergy were neither united nor unquestioned. This poem is also embedded in intertextual dialogue with a group of texts sharing its metrical structure, which all seem to present catechetical and penitential statements of faith attributed to the influence of the friars. It is worth considering the part that authorial intention can play in such intertextual dialogues, especially those informed by aggression.[32] As Margaret Rose points out: 'The parody can play upon the expectations of an imagined reader or recipient in the construction of its parody.' An important feature would be 'the parody's own internal evocation of the expectations of the reader',[33] for example in the form of a model that is both familiar and open to critique. The reader's expectation, as I hope to show, would have been of quite a different text to the one Peire presents. The text below is taken from Lavaud's edition; for the sake of clarity, I have divided the translation into paragraphs (*PC* 335, 64, Lavaud, XXXIV):

Un estribot farai, que er mot maïstratz,
De motz novels e d'al e de divinitatz.
Qu'ieu n'ai en Dieu crezenza que fon de maire natz,
D'una santa pieusela, per que.l mons es salvatz.
E es paire e filhs e santa trinitatz,
E es en tres personas e una unitatz.
E cre que.l cels e.l tros ne fos per el traucatz
E.n trabuquet los angels: can los trobet dampnatz.
E crey que sans Joans lo tenc entre sos bratz
E.l bateguet en l'aigua, et flum, can fo propchatz;
E conoc be la senha abanchas que fo natz:
El ventre de sa maire que.s volve al destre latz.
E cre Rom'e sant Peire a cuy fon comandatz
Jutge de penedensa, de sen e de foldatz.
Mas so non crezon clergue que fan las falcetatz,
Que son larc d'aver penre et escas de bontatz,
E son bel per la cara et ore de peccatz,
E devedon als autres d'aco que fan lur atz,
E en loc de matinas an us ordes trobatz
Que jazon ab putanas tro.l solelhs es levatz,
Enans canton baladas e prozels trasgitatz:
Abans conquerran Dieu Cayfas o Pilatz.

Monge solon estar dino los mostiers serratz
On azoravan Dieu denan las magestatz,
E can son en las vilas on an lurs poestatz,
Si avetz bela femna o es homs molheratz,
El seran cobertor, si.eus peza o si.eus platz;
E can el son desus e.l cons es sagelatz
Ab las bolas redondas que pendon al matratz,
Con las letras son clausas e lo traucs es serratz,
D'aqui eyson l'iretge e li essabataz
Que juron e renegon e jogon a tres datz:
Aiso fan monge negre en loc de caritatz.
Mon estribotz fenisc que es tot compassatz,
C'ai trag de gramatica e de divinitatz;
E si mal o ai dig, que.m sia perdonatz,
Que yeu o dic per Dieu, qu'en sia pus amatz,
  E per mal estribatz
    Clergues.

[I shall compose an *estribot*, which will be very 'mastered',[34] in new words and in others, and in theology. For I have faith in God, who was born of a mother, a holy virgin, through whom the world is saved. And He is Father and Son and Holy Trinity, and is in three persons, and one unity. And I believe that the sky and its vault were opened by Him, and that He cast down the angels, when He found them to be damned. And I believe that Saint John held Him in his arms and baptized Him in the water, in the river, when He drew near; and He knew well the sign before His birth, in the belly of His mother, which turned to the right. And I believe in Rome and Saint Peter, to whom it was commanded to judge repentance, sense and folly.

But the clerks don't believe this, who tell lies, who are generous in taking wealth, and tight-fisted in good deeds, and are handsome of face, but hideous with sin, who prohibit others from doing that which suits them, and who, in place of Matins, have found an order of service: that they should lie with whores until the sun has risen. Instead they sing *baladas* and travestied *prosae*: Caïaphas or Pilate would gain Paradise faster than them.

Monks used to stay locked in their chapels, where they worshipped God before holy statues; when they are in the towns where they have their leaders, if you have a beautiful wife, or are a married man, they will play the coverlet, whether you like it or not. And when they are on top, the cunt is sealed, with the round balls that hang from the spear, when the letters are closed and the hole is locked. From there come the heretics and the Waldensians, who swear and renegue and play with three dice. That's what black monks do in place of Charity.

I'll finish my *estribot*, which is measured with care, for I made it with grammar and theology; and if I've said bad things in it, may I be forgiven, for I said it for the sake of God, that He might be better loved, and for the badly 'estriboted'[35] Clerks.]

Only one other example survives of the *estribot*, a minor satirical genre which produced the Italian *strambotto*. First attested in the tenth century as a mocking song, it seems to have been viewed as a form of invective, 'Amb home janglayre, estribotayre ni escarnidor no deu hom gayre parlar' [With a jeering, *estribot*-making or scornful man one should not speak].[36] The other surviving piece is a nine-line fragment attributed to the troubadour Palais; also in alexandrines with the fixed rhyme '-uz', it describes a monk fornicating with a lady (*PC* 315, 5).[37]

The *estribot* is not split into stanzas. Its structure of monorhymed alexandrines ended by a six-syllable *cauda* is shared with the twelfth-century epic crusade narrative *Canso d'Antiocha*, which is the source for both parts of the *Chanson de la croisade albigeoise*.[38] The same metrical form is also used for several devotional texts from the thirteenth century: a *Vida* of Saint Amans, Raimon de Castelnou's *Doctrinal*, a pseudo-debate between a Cathar and a preacher called *Las Novas del Heretge*, and a penitential confession directly inspired by the repression of Catharism, all of which are written in alexandrine laisses linked by short *caudas capfinidas*. Peire de Courbian's *Thezaur* is also composed in monorhymed alexandrines, and may be joined to this group.

The Occitan epic laisse has been related to the Latin *prosa* by virtue of such examples as the neumed addition 'Dixit Domino Alleluia' to the manuscript of the *Chanson de Sainte Foi*, which implies that the text was sung to a melodic line borrowed from the Alleluia *melisma*, the formal basis of the *prosa*.[39] Meanwhile, the structural similarities cited above place the *estribot* in dialogue with a group of texts several of which focus on the negotiation of religious and political positions. This seems very germane to both the dating and the ideological position of Peire Cardenal's text. While the second part is closer to Peire's declared political opinions, the first part of the *Chanson de la croisade albigeoise* (composed by Guilhem de Tudela around 1210) shares the formal structure, historical context, interests and concerns of the *estribot*, but adopts a different political position. One passage in particular is worth citing here (laisses 45–6):[40]

A Tholosa intrè li abas de Cistel;
Mot s'en meravilheron li vialh e.l jovencel,
E li un e li autre, neis li petit tozel.
Vezentre tot lo poble lor livret lo castel,
C'anc hom en terra plana non vit, so cug, tan bel.
Mota carta n'an faita, mot breu e mot sagel,
Que le trames pel mon entro a Mon Gibel.
Li reis d'Arago I venc a lui de vas Murel,
E parlè ab dons abas en un prat, a Portel;
E anc no i delhivrero que valha un anel
De nulha avol fivela.

L'evesques de Tholosa, Folquets cel de Maselha,
Que degus de bontat ab el no s'aparelha,
E l'abas de Cistel l'us ab l'autre cosselha.
Tot jorn van prezican la gen co no.us revelha;
Del prest e del renou l'un e l'autre s'querelha.
Per trastot Agenes lor tenc aital roelha
Si qu'en cavalguet l'abas tro a Santa Bazelha.
Anc re preziquesson no mezon dins l'aurelha
Ans dizon per esquern: 'Ara roda l'abelha.'
Per qu'ieu, si m'ajud fes, no m'en fas meravelha
Si om be los confon, ni los rauba, ni.ls pelha,
Ni per forsa.ls castia.

[Into Toulouse came the abbot of Cîteaux; young and old were amazed, even the little children. Before the whole population, the Count handed over the castle to him, never was one so fine seen in a flat land, I think. They made many charters, many briefs and many sealed letters, that they took across the world, as far as to Mount Etna. The king of Aragon rode to him from near Muret, and spoke to the lord abbot in a meadow, at Portel; but they didn't even reach a wretched buckle's worth of conclusion.

The bishop of Toulouse, Folquet of Marseilles (no man was ever better) and the abbot of Cîteaux discussed with one another. All day they went preaching to people who slumbered on; they both condemned money-lenders and usury. They travelled throughout the Agenais, the abbot rode as far as Sainte-Bazeille. But the people didn't take in the things that they preached, but said, in mockery, 'Now the bee's droning'. God help me, that's why I, for one, am not surprised if they are defeated, robbed, pillaged or punished with force.]

Guillem de Tudela's text, Part I of the *Chanson de la croisade*, supports the Crusade and asserts that the people of the Languedoc have brought destruction upon themselves by ignoring preaching campaigns. Part II is hostile to the Crusade and to Folquet de Marselha, the bishop of Toulouse and former troubadour, but does not attack clerics in the text as violently as the *estribot*.

The *estribot* is an attack on clerks who do not practise what they preach. The term 'monges negres' usually refers to the Benedictine order, and seems to refer to an enclosed order who have turned to preaching (vv. 23–4). Lavaud suggests it may also have been used for Dominican friars, who were established in Toulouse from 1216, to stormy effect.[41] This suggestion is difficult to accept, since the text clearly refers to Benedictine habit and enclosure. It was, in fact, typical of mendicant attacks on monastic preaching to allege that silence was the proper action of a monk.[42] However, the text seems to refer to two groups, black monks and 'clergues' engaged in parallel activities. The attack on the Benedictines preaching in the city is set side-by-side with a more general attack on clerks, among whom Dominicans might be counted.

After an announcement that the poet will compose an *estribot* which will be 'maïstratz' and learned in both grammar and theology, the song then presents a *Credo* which refers to the Virgin Birth, the Trinity, the casting down of the fallen angels, the baptism of Christ and the role of John the Baptist.[43] There is explicit devotion to Rome and St Peter, which should invalidate any assumption that this text is composed by a supporter of heresy. Despite the speaker's claims to advanced theological knowledge, his knowledge of Scripture as he displays it could be based on sermons he has heard; for example, lines 11–12 describe the Visitation of Mary in terms similar to those chosen by a vernacular preacher, in MS Tortosa 106 (Thomas, XIII): 'ela entret en la maison de sca Helisabet e saludet la, e li enfant alegreron si els ventres de lurs maires e coneg l'uns l'altre' [she entered the house of St Elizabeth and greeted her, and the children rejoiced in the bellies of their mothers and recognized each other].

What is the purpose of this display of doctrine? The Treaty of Paris (1229) decreed that the new university of Toulouse should employ 'four masters of theology, two decretists, six masters of the liberal arts and two grammarians',[44] to improve the learning of the local population. Noted orators such as the Cistercian Hélinant de Froidmont were brought to Toulouse to instruct the population in correct doctrine, and to reinforce the preaching of the Dominican order. The speaker may be contrasting his own *divinitatz* with that imposed by the new arrivals.

From their cloistered existence and contemplation of holy images, monks have moved into urban life and acquired temporal power. This power is expressed through a complicated set of images in which the seduction of citizens' wives is equated with the signing and sealing of letters, which may be linked to the handing over of the city of Toulouse described in the passage above: the women are sealed 'con las letras', with letters and with learning, a mingling of written deeds with symbolic objects.[45] Rather than stamping out heresy through their preaching, these clerks spread erroneous readings of doctrine; in the poet's words, they father heretics, some of whom become heretical preachers. The poet ends with an assertion that his song is for the common good; it is theologically informed, and destined to correct the belief of those listening, and of the clerks who are its ultimate target and addressees.

The *clericus* in the twelfth and thirteenth centuries was a man defined by non-servile, non-warrior status, knowledge of the psalms, ability to sing the liturgical offices and tonsure.[46] Peire Cardenal wishes his targeted *clergues* were enclosed and contemplative, which implies a hostility towards the peripatetic careers opening up in the early thirteenth century, such as becoming a friar or teaching at a university.[47] Similarly, Peire's *sirventes* 'Ab votz d'angel' (*PC* 335, 1, XXVIII) depicts the Dominicans as smooth-tongued hypocrites whose skilful preaching is a mask for self-indulgence and lechery.

The content of the *estribot* is structured as a decline from the Trinity (v. 5) to the three dice of heretics (v. 32), with travestied liturgical tropes and travestied sacred knowledge at its centre (v. 21). Playing with three dice has been identified as a sexual metaphor by Bec, in relation to a *tenso* between Uguet and the *joglar* Reculaire (Bec, 2, *PC* 417, 1/458, 1), in which the latter brags:

> E jogui ab tres datz,
> E pren ab lo cons paria,
> Et ab bon vin, on que sia.
> (vv. 26–8)

[And I play with three dice, and pair up with the cunt, and with good wine, wherever it may be.]

At the start of the exchange, however, Uguet accuses Reculaire of being a Waldensian given to drinking, gambling and womanizing (vv. 3–4), which would suggest a stronger connection between heresy and the social vices listed in both these texts. Through this image, the decline from the spiritual to the carnal, emblematized in the cultivation of heresy and sinful vices, is shown to be complete.

This *estribot* is evidently ironic in its claim to be written to improve its addressees (vv. 36–9), for its promise of spiritual enlightenment at the start is ended by an obscene set of images destined to warn and denounce, not to teach. It attacks clerks for travestying liturgical songs, a comment which may be made about its own structure and approach, since the term 'prozels trasgitatz' occurs between the Credo and the increasingly aggressive attack that follows it. It may be argued that the *estribot* ultimately parodies itself, since by using a serious form associated with doctrinal teaching it presents a serious text, followed by an obscene *para*-text.

The satirical element of the *estribot* is undeniable, but its parodic basis makes its attack ambiguous. The positioning of the speaker becomes important at this point, especially given his own claims to being a clerk of mastered words and solid doctrinal knowledge. It begs the question of how different Peire Cardenal is from the *clergues* of this song, who also engage in *trobar* (v. 21) and leave the cloister to explore the secular pleasures of the city, experiencing success through the spoken and written word. These clerks are creating a chain of false words and false men, who will perpetuate their travesty of the sacred. By extension, the speaker's own *gramatica* and *divinitatz* may be no more true than that of the *clergues* he denounces.

A similar condemnation of a breach with a spiritual vocation can be found in an attack on the twelfth-century troubadour Peire d'Alvernha:

E quan canorgues si mes
Pey d'Alvernh'en canongia
a Dieu per que.s prometia
entiers que poys si fraysses?
Quar si feys, fols joglars es
per que l'entier pretz cambia.
(*PC* 63, 6, Beggiato V, vv. 31–6)

[And when Peire d'Alvernha became a canon in a canonry, why did he promise himself wholly to God if he was to break with him later? He's a foolish *joglar* for having done this, for he changed his whole worth.]

Earlier in this song, Bernart Marti attacks the lyric genres, including the *estribot*, as little more than deceit and lechery:

Foudat fai e nescies
qui vers fa de truandia,

pessan qu'entiers ni fragz sia:
que chanso ni sirventes
n'estribot ni arlotes
non es mas quan licharia.
(vv. 19–24)

[He does a foolish and stupid thing who makes a song out of lies, thinking it is either whole or broken: for a *canso*, a *sirventes*, an *estribot* or an *arlotes* are no more than lechery.]

For Bernart, there can be no recuperation by rhetoric or interpretation of secular *vers*. On one level, this song is evidence of a literary debate about poetics. On the other, it brings together disapproval, of the canon who breaks with his vocation, and of the act of composing frivolous songs. It is interesting that Bernart should concentrate on Peire d'Alvernha's past vocation as a canon, without specifying whether this indicates a canon of a regular order or a cathedral canon. According to Jacques Heers, the cathedral canons were the group of clergy most closely associated with the Feast of Fools and parodic activity.[48] Peire Cardenal was trained in a cathedral canonry, and may be expected to have participated in such rituals. Regular canons feature elsewhere in the troubadour corpus: Peire's contemporary Peire Rogier, who was also from the Auvergne and a canon at Clermont, is said to have left his religious house in order to earn fame as a *joglar* (*BS*, XL).

Whereas regular canons such as Peire Rogier were known to travel, study and practise secular literature, the later twelfth century saw repeated attempts to restrict their secular lives, and bring them into line with other regular clergy, especially from *c.*1214 onwards; southern canons were especially resistant to this move.[49] This oscillation between tolerance and repression is seen in the *vidas* of the canons Gui d'Ussel and Daude de Pradas (*BS*, XXII and XXX). Whereas Daude, who was active between *c.*1214 and *c.*1282, seems to have composed poetry and treatises on hawking without censure, Gui d'Ussel (fl. *c.*1195–*c.*1225) (*BS*, XXII) courted *domnas* and composed songs until the Papal legate forbade him doing so, upon which he gave up 'lo trobar e.l cantar'. As practitioners of secular poetry, Bernart claims that both he and Peire d'Alvernha have surrendered their claim to spiritual wholeness, and both must be humble in their overt commitment to worldly things. The fact that Peire d'Alvernha also composed devotional *vers* may indicate further tension about the issue of the secular lives of many canons. Indeed, Peire's satirical gallery of poets includes the comment that Peire Rogier would be better suited to reading from a psalter or carrying a candle than to singing about love in public (*PC* 323, 11, Zenker, XII, vv. 7–12). Peire Cardenal, a former canon who may have started his career as a troubadour before 1214, could have been implicated in the same association with parodic activity, and the same moral unease.

There is also a possibility that the *estribot* may be a parody of other propaganda texts dealing with the religious persecution in the Toulousain in the early part of the thirteenth century. Three texts sharing the metre and structure of the *estribot* are closely interlinked. *Las Novas del Heretge* stages the confession and repentance of a Cathar bishop through the preaching of inquisitors. A confessional prayer composed in the same form, 'Dona sancta', depicts the rejection of heresy by an anonymous penitent who credits inquisitors with his conversion. There is also Raimon de Castelnou's *Doctrinal*, a religious *ensenhamen* inspired by 'bons clercs' who may be friars, which the author presents as a text destined to be memorized and used to improve the faith of those who learn it. One of the two versions of the *Doctrinal* is preserved in the same manuscript as 'Dona sancta', British Museum Harley 7403, a fourteenth-century codex from the Narbonne area. All the texts cited above include transparent praise of the order of preachers, the inquisitors and those bishops who co-operated with their investigations.

Raimon's text, which is structured in fourteen laisses, 400 lines long in all, opens with a formal statement of faith, and presents itself generically as a *doctrinal* both at the start and the end:[50]

> E nom de dieu lo paire e de la trinitat
> e de la dousa verge que Jhesu a portat
> comens un doctrinal que es tot de vertat.
> (MS BM Harley 7403, f. 111)

[In the name of God the father and of the Trinity, and of the sweet Virgin who bore Jesus, I begin a *Doctrinal*, which is made all of truth.]

Apart from the obvious intertextual relationship between this opening and that of the *estribot*, the *Doctrinal* shares the metre of the *estribot*, and begins and ends on the fixed rhyme '-at' or '-atz' (laisses 1, 3 and 14). Raimon states that his text is a work of penitence for the 'crois cantars' [wicked songs] of his past (v. 153), and wishes that it should be read aloud regularly, even daily, in order to teach his listeners correct doctrine (vv. 375–9). This is directly followed by a defensive passage, in which Raimon appears both to deny the influence of clerical learning on his text, and to endorse it as the source of his *doctrina*. This passage seems to anticipate the criticism of an audience apt to deride his words as those of a disguised clerical propagandist, and is intent on naming the speaker as the sole author, albeit with assistance, of the text:

> E negus hom nos pesse qu'ieu sia hom letratz,
> an[s], son us cavaliers laicx de paucas heretatz:
> Raimon de Castelnou so[n] per nom apellat[z],
> pero per de bons clercs ne ssoy endoutrinat[z];
> qu'estiers, non pogra aver tant de dit[z] ajustatz.[51]
> (vv. 388–92)

[And let no man think I am a learned man; for I am a lay knight of poor origins: Raimon de Castelnou is my name, but I have been indoctrinated by good clerks, for I could never have put so many stories together alone.]

Raimon ends the poem with an exhortation to listen, and to follow the text with a humble prayer of penitence, which will absolve both him and his listeners of their sins (vv. 387–94).

The ending of the *Doctrinal* is similar to the closure of 'Dona sancta', the confessional prayer which precedes it in Harley 7403, which Nelli interprets as the penitential work of a former Cathar, composed soon after 1242.[52] This text, which is in nineteen laisses, 839 lines long, seems to address an audience of people who have indoctrinated its speaker, and ends with the following dedication:

> Ferms estau en la fe e ferms m'i a trobat
> L'avesque G.P. ab cui iei comversat,
> Fraire B. de Caux c'a mos amicx estat
> E fraire P. Cenres c'a mest nos predicat.
> De fraire A. vos dic que agui.l cor irat
> Car si parti de nos ab aital comiat.
> D'aquels II.II per nom ai ieu penedensat,
> Segon que mi sentia de mal ni de pecat,
> Per que prec Jhesu Crist qu'el me do s'amistat.
> Amen. Amen. Amen.
> (vv. 830–9)

[I was firm in the faith and firm they found me, bishop G. P. with whom I lived, brother B. of Caux who was my friend, brother P. Cenres who preached among us. About brother A., I tell you I had a saddened heart when he took such leave of us. From these four I have named I took penance, according to the evil and sin I felt were in me, which is why I pray Jesus Christ he might grant me his friendship, Amen, amen, amen!][53]

Set against the *estribot*, this confession and the *doctrinal* appear to be ideal targets for Peire Cardenal's mockery. Like the Toulousain congregations muttering about buzzing bees, Peire's song appears to call the bluff of a layman who may claim to be speaking as a mere knight and penitent, but who has a clearly articulated agenda and admits that his words are in part dictated by 'bons clercs'. The *doctrinal* is a catechetical text presented as a piece to be heard daily, in order to inculcate doctrinal conformity into its listeners. Its author is himself the product of this teaching (v. 385) and adopts a penitential position, suggesting that his listeners should follow the path he has already taken (vv. 11–15).

Similarly, the anonymous penitent speaking in 'Dona sancta' is not a newly reformed heretic. He notes that any attraction he might once have found in heresy was stamped out of him by 'the good sense of my mother' over forty years beforehand (vv. 826–7), a rejection maintained by the Dominicans and inquisitors he names. In fact, he reveals in what may be a slip of the pen that he is a preacher himself: 'Ni volon nostre creire que lur avem monstrat' (v. 816) [Nor do they wish to believe our ideas that we have demonstrated to them]. His rejection of dualism is certainly not spontaneous, and could be described as a carefully crafted piece of rhetoric. I would have to disagree with Nelli's reading of the text, and suggest that it is not the work of a repentant heretic, but of a layman presenting the ideas of the inquisitors he accompanies to a lay audience.

Peire Cardenal's *estribot* attacks the preachers who have inspired these texts, alleging that they spread their doctrine in order to serve their own interests; according to him, they are creating 'false' preachers, laymen who may spread inaccurate views of doctrine. Given the probable date of the *doctrinal* (*c.*1229), Raimon's text seems to be the likeliest target for Peire Cardenal's parody, a suggestion reinforced by the existence of a direct intertextual relationship between the two poets, in the *sirventes* 'Mon chantars vueil retraire al cuminal' (*PC* 396, 6 or 335, 37, Lavaud, LX), which is attributed to both troubadours. The content of the fourth stanza of this *sirventes* is strikingly similar to that of the *estribot* (the text is from Beltran's edition):[54]

Si monge nier uol Dieus que sian sal
per pro manjar ni per femnas tenir
ni monge blanc per boulas amentir
ni per erguelh Temple ni l'Ospital
ni canonge per prestar a renieu,
ben tenc per folh sant Peir' e Sanh Andrieu
que sofriro per Dieu aital turmen
s'aquest se.n uan aissi a saluamen.

(vv. 25–32)

[If God wishes the black monks to be saved by eating well and keeping women, or the white monks by falsifying boundaries, or by the pride of the [Orders of the] Temple and Hospital, or by canons practising loans for usury, I consider Saint Peter and Saint Andrew to have been fools indeed, for suffering such torment for God, if these men reach salvation in this way.]

Could this be one of the 'crois cantars' Raimon has set aside?

To summarize this discussion, Peire Cardenal's *estribot* may be read as a direct parody of a specific text, the *doctrinal* of Raimon de Castelnou, which it attacks for making specious claims to truth in terms of secular piety inspired by preaching. The song may also depict the usurpation of language and power by the French nobility and the attached preaching campaigns by various groups of enclosed and mendicant clergy. It may also comment on the complexity of judging the activities of secular, defrocked and ordained clerks, especially in terms of their claims to sincerity in teaching doctrine.

To say that it is possible to learn the hypotext (the model) from the hypertext (the parody) is a long-established but disputed aspect of studies of parody.[55] Peire's *estribot* presents a Credo as well as a set of implied precepts for men in religious orders. However, it would be difficult to read it as a didactic text in the same vein as Raimon de Castelnou's, which also presents the Credo as part of its catechetical programme. Peire's speaker claims to be a true believer who is shocked by the flouting of doctrine on the part of the *clergues*; yet he also depicts their activities in metaphorical terms, combining comic with aesthetic effect. Beyond the basic level of parodic aggression, which appears to challenge the 'bons clercs' cited by Raimon as his teachers, the text is also a display of outrageous comic invention. Ultimately, the poem is read not in terms of its devotional content, but in the way it distorts, secularizes and profanes it. It is, in itself, an example of *prozels trasgitatz*.

The reductive performance of parody may oscillate between

buffoonery and pamphleteering within a given text, with the appeal to social consensus marking out the license allowed the speaker. The rest of this study will be devoted to a chain of parodies which, unlike the texts examined above, do not carry elements of political conflict. They are texts which engage in a complex dialogue, in which parody, debasement, recuperation and intertextual play play key roles. The oscillation between 'repetition with critical distance' and reductive aggression can be illustrated in these texts, all of which, at some level, refer to a sacred model. As Jacques Heers suggests, 'la fête comique, burlesque, donc très vite satirique, est, par origine et par essence, paraliturgique: des divertissements d'initiés pour surprendre les autres, les choquer même, puis tenter de les entraîner'.[56] Since many troubadours were 'initiés', the extent of the shock value of their parodies will be bound to their capacity to draw the audience into their game, if such it was.

One problem that remains unaddressed is how the audience and performers would have received the ludic reduction of texts overtly presented as sacred or didactic, outside immediate questions of political conflict. It is tempting to read such texts as purely ludic on the grounds that the medieval tradition of carnival made anti-clerical humour acceptable.[57] In his famous essay on carnival, Bakhtin notes that in 'the further development of humorous Latin literature, parodical doublets of every ecclesiastical cult and teaching were created—the so-called *parodia sacra*, "sacred parody", one of the most peculiar and least understood manifestations of medieval literature'. His explanation for the existence of these ambiguous texts is that 'all this was consecrated by tradition and, to a certain extent, tolerated by the Church [...] it was in part directly linked, as in the parodies of liturgies and prayers, with the "feast of fools" and may have been performed during this celebration'.[58]

Bakhtin's view of carnival (or the use made of it by others) has been criticized as anachronistic. To read parodies produced in the Middle Ages exclusively in terms of annual moments of licensed steam-letting in a calendar of pious observance produces a potent template, but one which effectively neutralizes the power of such texts as Peire Cardenal's. The *estribot* becomes a 'mere' instance of licensed parody to be pigeon-holed with boy bishops, asses' masses and court jesters, and its political implications may be set aside. However, the proximity of the *estribot* to a set of propagandist texts indicates that its historical context cannot be dismissed so easily.

A further drawback of accepting all carnivalization as purely ludic is that it confirms an 'Age of Faith' reading of the Middle Ages, as a culture in which ecclesiastical hierarchy and doctrine were never truly questioned.[59] On the contrary, parody of the sacred may be received either as licensed comment or as threatening provocation, depending on the context in which it is performed. For example, in 1445, the bishop of Troyes had two clerks tried for heresy, for having displayed a defamatory tract against him after he invited a Parisian theologian to preach against their Feast of Fools.[60] If the religious establishment of the time perceived the Feast of Fools and its defenders as potential heretics, this would compromise the Bakhtinian view of the *Risus Natalis* as a mere licensed safety-valve. On the other hand, the case may be purely the product of power struggles within the diocese, and the accusation of heresy a convenient mask for disciplinary action.[61]

Another example may be found in the marginalia of Psalters and Bibles, where the juxtaposition of obscene sexual and spiritual images is undeniably contained and ludic, but may contain the seeds of polemic as '*conscious* usurpations, perhaps even political statements about diffusing the power of the text through its unravelling'.[62] However, jokes offering no valid alternative to the dominant culture are ultimately supportive of it, which makes carnival complicitous with power: it is inevitably the marginal illustration of the central image, text or city to which it owes its existence.[63] A parodic work with satirical elements may depend on the degree of 'license to criticize' allotted the speaker, who often depended on the favour of a patron, or on the favour of the audience or readers addressed.

If we assume that distortion of the sacred was a gesture of intimacy rather than of defiance, this reading makes it possible to suppose that series of parodies composed in this period, such as the chain of texts which will be studied below, should end with a serious rewriting with difference, in the form of a sermon.

Such chains of *hypertextes* (to use Genette's term, which denotes the simultaneous presence, acknowledged or not, of one text within another)[64] deploy equal amounts of debunking and recuperation. Licensed parody of the sacred implies that such activity has a political dimension which acquires visibility only once the institution being parodied perceives such textual aggression as valid opposition, rather than a mere joke. It could be that Peire's suspicion of parodic activity stems from his immersion in a context—thirteenth-century Languedoc—that was informed by intense conflict over the authority of the church and its speech. The texts I shall examine in the next five chapters appear to arise from a less conflictual social context, but one in which the relationship between texts is still marked by combat, competition and recuperative strategies.

Notes to Chapter 1

1. Jacques Chailley, *L'Ecole musicale de Saint-Martial-de-Limoges, jusqu'à la fin du XIe siècle* (Paris: Les livres essentiels, 1960); Margaret Switten, 'Modèle et variations: Saint Martial-de-Limoges et les troubadours', *Contacts de langues, de civilisations et intertextualité: Actes du IIIe Congrès international de l'Association Internationale d'Etudes Occitanes, Montpellier, 20–26 septembre 1990*, ed. Gérard Gouiran, 3 vols. (Montpellier: Centre d'Etudes Occitanes de l'Université de Montpellier, 1992), ii. 679–96.
2. Ruth E. Harvey, '*Joglars* and the professional status of the early troubadours', *Medium Aevum* 62 (1993), 221–41.
3. Lavaud, *Peire Cardenal*, 106–7.
4. *R*, iii. 471; *PSW*, viii. 386.
5. Bec, *Burlesque*, 10 n.; Peter Linehan, *The Ladies of Zamora* (Manchester: Manchester University Press, 1997), 48–52.
6. James Grier, 'A New Voice in the Monastery: Tropes and Versus from Eleventh- and Twelfth-Century Aquitaine', *Speculum* 69 (1994), 1023–69 (1036).
7. Diego Zorzi, *Valori religiosi nella letteratura provenzale: la spiritualità trinitaria* (Milan: Società editrice "Vita e Pensiero", 1954), 38–9.
8. Alfred Jeanroy and Giulio Bertoni, 'Le *Thezaur* de Peire de Courbian', *Annales du Midi* 23 (1921), 290–400; Zorzi, *Valori religiosi*, 140–2.
9. John Stevens, *Words and Music in the Middle Ages* (Cambridge: Cambridge University Press, 1986), 505–11.
10. Jacques Heers, *Fêtes des fous et carnavals au Moyen Age* (Paris: du Seuil, 1978), 75–104; Stevens, *Words and Music*, 178–86.
11. Heers, *Fêtes des fous*, 43.
12. Paul Lehmann, *Die Parodie im Mittelalter* (Munich: Drei Masken Verlag, 1922); Martha Bayless, *Parody in the Middle Ages: The Latin Tradition* (Ann Arbor: University of Michigan Press, 1996).
13. Heers, *Fêtes des fous*, 88–91.
14. Sanda Golopentia-Eretescu, 'La parodie et la feinte', in *Dire la Parodie: Actes du Colloque de Cerisy*, ed. Clive Thomson and Armand Pagès (Bern: Peter Lang, 1989), 35–66 (37).
15. Heers, *Fêtes des fous*, 38.
16. Gérard Genette, *Palimpsestes: La littérature au second degré* (Paris: Seuil, 1982), 19–68; Margaret Rose, *Parody: Ancient, Modern and Post-Modern* (Cambridge: Cambridge University Press, 1993), 37–46.
17. Linda Hutcheon, *A Theory of Parody: The Teachings of Twentieth-Century Art Forms* (London: Methuen, 1985), 6.

18. See my article, 'Defamation in the Troubadour *Sirventes*: Legislation and Troubadour Poetry', *Medium Ævum* 66 (1997), 28–41; Jean Duvernoy, *Registre d'inquisition de Jacques Fournier (1318–1325)*, 3 vols. (Toulouse: Privat, 1965), iii. 318–20, 328–9.
19. Kathryn Gravdal, *Vilain et Courtois: Transgressive Parody in French Literature of the Twelfth Century* (Lincoln, NE: University of Nebraska Press, 1989), 5–11.
20. Martín de Riquer, *Los Trovadores*, iii. 1270–9; 'Flors de Paradis', in *La lírica religiosa en la literatura provenzal antigua: edición crítica, traducción, notas y glosario*, ed. Francisco Oroz Arizcuren (Pamplona: Disputación foral de Navarra, institución principal de Viana, 1972).
21. Katherina Städtler, 'The *Sirventes* by Gormonda de Montpeslier', in *The Voice of the Trobairitz: Perspectives on the Women Troubadours*, ed. William D. Paden (Philadelphia: Pennsylvania University Press, 1989), 129–37.
22. See de Riquer, *Los Trovadores*, iii. 1270.
23. Bayless, *Parody in the Middle Ages*, 93–4.
24. Hutcheon, *A Theory of Parody*, 64–5.
25. Rose, *Parody*, 40–2.
26. Lehmann, *Die Parodie im Mittelalter*, 13–14, 119.
27. Bayless, *Parody in the Middle Ages*, 3–4.
28. Hutcheon, *Theory of Parody*, 53–68.
29. Genette, *Palimpsestes*, 12–16, 18–19.
30. Hutcheon, *Theory of Parody*, 80–4.
31. Ruth E. Harvey, 'The satirical use of the courtly expression *sidons* in the works of the troubadour Marcabru', *MLR* 78 (1983), 24–33, and *The Troubadour Marcabru and Love*. But see also Gaunt, 'Marginal Men'.
32. See Elizabeth W. Poe, '*Pos podetz las rimas seguir contrasemblantz*: Imitators of the Master Troubadour Giraut de Bornelh', in *The Medieval 'Opus': Imitation, Rewriting, and Transmission in the French Tradition. Proceedings of the Symposium held at the Institute for Research in the Humanities, October 5–7 1995, the University of Wisconsin—Madison*, ed. Douglas Kelly (Amsterdam and Atlanta: Rodopi, 1997), 279–97.
33. Rose, *Parody*, 39.
34. *PSW*, v. 7–12; *R*, iv. 118; *PD*, 230.
35. *PSW*, iii. 349; *R*, iii. 231.
36. Peter Ricketts, 'L'Estribot, forme et fond', *Mélanges de langue et de littérature occitanes en hommage à Pierre Bec* (Poitiers: Université de Poitiers, CESCM, 1991), 475–83 (477).
37. See Sergio Vatteroni, 'Peire Cardenal e l'*estribot* nella poesia provenzale', *Medioevo Romanzo* 15 (1990), 61–91, and Ricketts, 'L'Estribot'.
38. Frank, *Répertoire métrique*, ii. 74, cites thirteen examples.
39. Robert Lafont, 'Pour rendre à l'oc et aux Normans leur dû: genèse et premier développement de l'art épique gallo-roman', *CCM* 42 (1999), 139–78 (157–9).
40. Guillem de Tudela and anon., *La Chanson de la Croisade Albigeoise*, ed. Eugène Martin-Chabot, trans. Henri Gougaud (Paris: Librairie Générale Française, 1989), 92.
41. Walter L. Wakefield, *Heresy, Crusade and Inquisition in Southern France, 1100–1250* (London: Allen and Unwin, 1974).
42. I would like to thank Carolyn Muessig for clarification of this point.

43. See also Peire de Courbian's *Thezaur*, vv. 165–70; Zorzi, *Valori religiosi*, 197.
44. Cyril Smith, *The University of Toulouse in the Middle Ages* (Milwaukee: Marquette University Press, 1958), 51–4.
45. See Michael Clanchy, *From Memory to Written Record: England 1066–1307* (London: Edward Arnold, 1979), 17–37, 202–6.
46. Clanchy, *From Memory to Written Record*, 175–201; Heers, *Fêtes des fous*, 31–2.
47. Alexander Murray, *Reason and Society in the Middle Ages* (Oxford: Clarendon Press, 1978), 218–33.
48. Heers, *Fêtes des fous*, 75–104.
49. Linda Paterson, *The World of the Troubadours: Medieval Occitan Society, 1100–1300* (Cambridge: Cambridge University Press, 1993), 318–19.
50. Andrea Giannetti (ed.), *Raimon de Castelnou: Canzoni e dottrinale* (Bari: Adriatica, 1988), 121–62.
51. Text from Giannetti, only in MS Florence, Bibl. Laurenziana, Ashburnham 40b.
52. René Nelli, *Ecrivains anticonformistes du moyen âge occitan, II. Hérétiques et politiques* (Paris: Phébus, 1977), 51–61 (54).
53. Nelli, *Ecrivains anticonformistes*, 61.
54. Vincenç Beltran, 'Tipos y temas trovadorescos. XIV. Alfonso X, Raimon de Castelnou y la corte literaria de Rodez', *Le Rayonnement des troubadours: Actes du Colloque de l'Association Internationale d'Etudes Occitanes, Amsterdam, 16–18 octobre 1995*, ed. Anton Touber (Amsterdam and Atlanta: Rodopi, 1998), 19–39.
55. Rose, *Parody*, and Genette, *Palimpsestes*; but see Grivel, 'Le retournement parodique', 8–9.
56. Heers, *Fêtes des fous*, 38.
57. Bakhtin, *Rabelais and his World*. See Rose, *Parody*, 125–70.
58. Bakhtin, *Rabelais and his World*, 14.
59. See Martin J. Schubert, 'Parody in Thirteenth-Century German Poetry', in *Parody: Dimensions and Perspectives*, ed. Müller, 237–73, 242–7.
60. Christelle Walravens, 'Insultes, blasphèmes ou hérésie? Un procès à l'officialité épiscopale de Troyes en 1445', *Bibliothèque de l'Ecole des Chartes* 154 (1996), 485–507; Heers, *Fêtes des fous*, 182–3.
61. Walravens, 'Insultes, blasphèmes ou hérésie?', 498–9.
62. Michael Camille, *Image on the Edge: The Margins of Medieval Art* (London: Reaktion Books, 1992), 42, 143–6.
63. Camille, *Image on the Edge*, 43–7; Stephen Greenblatt, 'Filthy Rites', in id. *Learning to Curse: Essays in Early Modern Culture* (New York and London: Routledge, 1990), 59–79 (73–4).
64. Genette, *Palimpsestes*, 12–16, 18–19.

CHAPTER 2

Metrical Structures and Formal Recognition

In his edition of Marcabru's boasting song (*gap*) 'D'aisso lau Deu' (*PC* 293, 16, Dejeanne, XVI), Aurelio Roncaglia describes the poem as 'un' amara parodia polemica'.[1] The term 'parody' implies a model, which Roncaglia provides in the form of a vernacular prayer to the Virgin found in the *marginalia* of a twelfth-century manuscript otherwise concerned with Roman satire, Paris BN lat. 11312 (formerly suppl. lat. 1743), f. 122^{v}:

> Prega sa jus
> lo pair de sus
> que lor fasa perdonament;
> mostra·l bos om
> que aital fasa om
> se l'autre·l fa malmenament.[2]

[Pray here below to the Father above, that he may forgive them; the good man shows that one should behave in this way, if another mistreats him.]

The *gap* appears to owe its metrical structure (448448, aabccb) to this poem. However, this 'stanza' is in fact a fragment extracted from a continuous piece, which is otherwise mostly in hexasyllables. The poem seems to be in two consecutive parts, and shifts between regular hexasyllables (most consistently in vv. 1–6, 28–42, 70–9) and a scheme of 446 or 448 (vv. 7–27, 43–69, with breaks), after a preface of four alexandrines. Meyer noted that the scribe had not attempted to indicate breaks in the text: 'les vers y sont transmis à la file, comme de la prose, sans aucun alinéa qui permette de reconnaître s'il n'y a qu'une seule pièce ou s'il faut en distinguer deux'.[3] His edition attempts to normalize the irregular layout of the text in the manuscript which, when transcribed without alteration to its form, reads quite differently:

> prega sa ius lo par de sus qe lor fasa perdonament .
> mostra.l bos om que aital fasa om se autre.l fa malmenament .

This isolated fragment from a much longer and more complex poem is only similar to 'D'aisso lau Deu' because of its implicit metrical structure of 448448. Its content bears no relation to the *gap*'s ironizing display of proprietal and sexual transgressions, and it seems highly unlikely that Marcabru's song could be a parody of this non-stanzaic prayer.

The answer to this problem lies in the metrical structure itself. Both Marcabru's poem and this fragment are in a form of versification known as the *versus tripertitus caudatus*, also called *strophe couée* or tail-rhyme.[4] This was a series of three-line versicles, independent units made up of a rhyming couplet followed by a tail-rhyme which linked one versicle to the next:

> Deus, receb me,
> qu'eu.m ret a te
> cofes e penent des pecaz.

[God, receive me, for I surrender myself to you, confessed and repentant of my sins.]

The versicle aab could be followed either by aab, or by ccb. These individual versicles gradually joined up and formed parallel groups, which eventually came to be regarded as stanzaic units. From aab, ccb, these became aabccb. The parallel groups created by fusion or pairing of three-line versicles may be seen in the archaic form of the liturgical sequence, also known as the Notkerian or irregular sequence. The division of pairs of versicles into stanzas appears in the later, or Victorine, sequence, thought to have developed at the beginning of the twelfth century. This form is also found in the vernacular, in Anglo-Norman didactic and narrative texts from the twelfth to thirteenth centuries, as well as in a number of troubadour songs and versified sermons. Given the predilection for the *versus tripertitus caudatus* in vernacular texts with devotional or didactic content, it seems likely that Marcabru's song is the 'bitter parody' of a liturgical model; its reception may depend on an audience primed to expect devotional content when associated with this metrical form. It would be helpful, moreover, to relate this song to texts composed in the *strophe couée* throughout.

The troubadour lyric is generally assumed to be a genre structurally predicated on the stanza as its basic unit, but the *versus tripertitus caudatus* is by definition a chain of three-line versicles, characterized in the Latin liturgical sequence by a responsion structure. The use of this metrical structure in troubadour song may, as a result, imply a challenge to assumptions about single-voiced performance and stanzaic structuring of texts. It also associates certain songs not with the *versus*, but with the sequence, specifically the *Alleluia* melisma and its associated tropes. This issue raises a further question about the relationship between the recognition of form according to discursive context, and the possibility of debate implicit in the choice of specific metrical structures in the troubadour lyric.

One supporting argument for this possible parodic relationship has been presented by Maria Luisa Meneghetti in her interpretation of the two scabrous 'Estornels' poems by Marcabru as a parody of a bilingual sequence to the Virgin from Saint-Martial-de-Limoges, 'In hoc anni circulo' (Paris BN fr. 1139), which may in turn have been modelled on a Hispano-Arabic *muwashshah*.[5] The text is famous for its alternating *coblas* in Occitan, which have been interpreted as early evidence of troubadour lyric threaded into a Latin hymn. 'In hoc anni circulo/ Mei amic e mei fiel' is not an isolated example in the Saint-Martial repertoire. Another vernacular song, 'O Maria Deu maire', has been identified as an adaptation of the famous hymn, 'Ave maris stella'.[6] Both texts point to a lively dialogue between Latin and vernacular sacred composition in the eleventh century.

There is evidence that Marcabru's poetic corpus is, at least in part, an instance of both local and formal or generic parody, addressing both his predecessors and the body of didactic and spiritual texts associated with these metrical structures. Study of the intertextual relationship between Marcabru and Guilhem IX[7] has emphasized the aggressivity of Marcabru's polemical readings of the first extant troubadour, who was also the father of his own initial patron, Guilhem X of Aquitaine (d. 1137). As textual parody, Marcabru's 'D'aisso lau Deu' is composed in opposition to the *amor de cavalher* of Guilhem IX, as displayed in his *companho* poems (*PC* 183, 3–5, Pasero, I–III), which are also composed in a form of the *versus tripertitus caudatus*, aaa, 11 11 14 (Frank, I, 1. 1–3). In his edition of Guilhem IX, Pasero proposes two competing formats for song *PC* 183, 3, as either 11a 11a 14a, or:

3b + 4b + 4a
3c + 4c + 4a
3d + 4d + 7a

This alternative structure makes it possible to relate this song to yet another polemical poem by Marcabru, 'En abriu' (*PC* 293, 24, Dejeanne, XXIV).[8]

If Guilhem IX parodied liturgical and para-liturgical models, it may be that Marcabru uses the same device to parody both Guilhem IX's celebrations of debauchery, and the devotional model initially attacked. Furthermore, 'D'aisso lau Deu' is itself parodied by Peire d'Alvernha in a later song, which appears to be a serious or spiritual parody of the *gap*. These texts are caught up in a chain of parodies, counter-parodies, *contrafacta* and ideological recuperations, which seems to end with a versified sermon attributed to Peire Cardenal, a member of the last two generations of troubadours. The chain of related texts in the *strophe couée* begins with the first extant troubadour in around 1100, and ends at the latest possible point in the years around 1275.

The form that has been identified as the basis for the metrical structures shared by one group of songs is the *versus tripertitus caudatus*. The greatest number of surviving examples of this form are in the rhymed Latin sequence, and in didactic vernacular texts, such as the Anglo-Norman *Disticha Catonis*.[9] One Occitan text that has been linked to this corpus is the anonymous *Arlabecca*, a versified mini-sermon which seems to intend to impress its audience with its shared homiletic and lyric character, and is written in an unusual form:[10]

Dieus vos salve trastotz essems:
Que sis fara verayamens,
  Si us non pecca,
Et entendes una arlabecca
Que ieu vos vuelh dire;
Sabes, no.m puesc chantar ni rire
  Ni far conortz:
Tan veg en poder de la mortz
  Tota la gen. (vv. 1–9)

[God save you all together! For this will he do truly, if one of you doesn't sin, and listen to an *arlabecca* I wish to recite to you; know that I cannot sing or laugh, nor amuse myself, so much do I see all people in the grip of death.]

Satirical Latin and vernacular poems composed in the *versus tripertitus caudatus* could have played on an effect of aesthetic rupture with a devotional model not dissimilar to that described by Suzanne Thiolier-Méjean with reference to the Occitan *sirventes*.[11] According to Thiolier-Méjean, the *sirventes*, by usurping a melody from an existing *canso*, and replacing the text with a provocative, disturbing or aggressive song, plays on a break with the audience's expectations. This theory is not without its flaws; Méjean cites examples from Marcabru, who does not seem to have borrowed melodies, since this *contrafactum* technique emerges only from the work of Bertran de Born (*c.*1160–*c.*1196) onwards. However, its basic premise, that troubadour satirical lyric aims to shock aesthetically as well as in terms of its content, is useful for this study. Rather than constituting a rupture with the *canso* (which is not associated with the *versus tripertitus caudatus*), this body of satirical and didactic songs plays on a rupture with liturgical texts, and para-liturgical chant, in form, language and content. The use of the vernacular may also have constituted an initial break with expectations in performance, when audiences would have heard the opening of a Latin chant, only to have it shift into a different language and register.

Parody depends on a similar mechanism, playing on the disjunction between the imitated text and its *détournement* to serve unexpected ends. Marcabru's *gap* uses both aesthetic and thematic rupture to surprise its audience, and bring into question both the Latin sequence and the poems of Guilhem IX. Rupture does not simply attack an expected utterance; it may also be produced by a movement away from, and therefore a comment upon, a specific context of utterance. Whether this break represents subversion of ecclesiastical discourse or its translation into a secular frame of reference will be examined later; first, evidence of such rupture must be traced in the liturgy and in the Occitan lyric corpus.

Richard Goddard's examination of surviving documents associated with Guilhem IX has suggested that the Duke of Aquitaine's relations with local ecclesiastical foundations and figures were not as strained as has previously been supposed.[12] While political activity is not necessarily a statement of ideological or religious commitment, it is worth considering that the defiance of Latin and clerical hegemony traced in his poetry by Laura Kendrick and others is undercut by an acceptance of this authority on an everyday level.[13] The hostility of later chroniclers, who depicted the Duke as an irreverently anti-clerical womanizer, has proved more attractive to a modern sensibility than evidence of his support of monastic houses. Guilhem IX's formal parody of para-liturgical chant may therefore be as double-edged as many other aspects of his corpus, both aggressive and supportive towards its object.

It will be useful to examine an instance of explicit parody, with an extant model text. Marcabru's 'D'aisso lau Deu' (Dejeanne, XVI) may parody Guilhem IX, but it also has a serious parody in 'Be m'es plazen', composed by a poet of the following generation, Peire d'Alvernha (Zenker, XII), which will be analysed later. Marcabru's song opens with a parodic invocation to God and St Andrew, which may make it a parody of a hymn, but no precise model has been found. However, the possibility of a shared para-liturgical model may be followed up not in terms of content, but in terms of form, in the metrical scheme adopted by both poets. It is also worth mentioning that the feast of St Andrew (30 November), like that of St John, was associated with pagan fertility rituals.[14] It is possible that Marcabru's erotic song plays on the dual significance—sacred and sexual—of the saint's day.

Both Marcabru and Peire use the metrical form 448448, aabccb, which appears reasonably frequently in tropers and collections of liturgical song in the analogous form 447447. It is, as Dronke defines it, 'a rhythmic trochaic tetrameter with caesura after the fourth and eighth syllables—a form much loved in early Christian poetry—[...] enriched by internal and final rhyme'.[15] For example, a Victorine sequence includes an isolated stanza in this metre:

Adam vetus
Tandem laetus
Novum promet canticum.
Fugitivus
Et captivus
Prodeat in publicum.[16]

[Old Adam, glad at last, will give a new song. A fugitive, a captive, let him step forward in public!]

The most likely candidate for a sequence borrowed by troubadours would be one contained in a Saint-Martial-de-Limoges manuscript, and preferably one designed for performance in liturgies accessible to a wider public. A striking example of such a piece can be found in the eleventh-century liturgical drama, the *Ordo prophetarum*, contained in Paris BN lat. 1139, ff. 55^{v}–58, after the more famous *Sponsus*.[17] Composed for performance at major liturgical feasts, these pieces were sung throughout in a semblance of dialogue; they seem to have been in use in the Limousin, and in places as far away as Laon. The *Ordo Prophetarum* can be located precisely, as it is a version of the Procession of the Prophets, a ceremony based on the eighth chapter of the pseudo-

Augustinian sermon 'Contra Judeos, Paganos, et Arianos' which was read at Matins during the Christmas season. This aggressively polemical text, which was occasionally parodied in the later Middle Ages, cites the words of Old Testament prophets as witnesses to the coming of Christ, and includes the Sybilline prophecy.[18] The *Ordo prophetarum* has a diverse range of metrical schemes, but tends to adhere to the aabccb, 448448 form more closely:

> Omnes gentes
> Congaudentes
> dent cantum leticie:
> Deus homo
> fit, de domo
> David natus hodie.
> (vv. 1–6)

[Let all the people rejoicing together offer a song of gladness: God is made man, born today of the house of David.]

In Laon, the *Ordo prophetarum* was performed by costumed actors, with appearances by the prophets Isaiah, Jeremiah and Daniel, as well as John the Baptist, Elizabeth, Virgil and the Erythrean Sybil.[19] The combination of costume, music and performance on a major feast-day all point to the *Ordo prophetarum* as an example of para-liturgical composition that would have been accessible to receptors outside the clergy. As a dramatic musical spectacle performed during Christmas offices, probably watched by secular audiences, the *Ordo*'s inclusion of a metrical scheme and melody that fit Marcabru's 'D'aisso lau Dieu' makes it a very likely model for subsequent parody.

However, the chief drawback of citing the *Ordo prophetarum* as a model lies in its content, which seems to be unrelated to that of the songs which are likely to have borrowed the melody. *Contrafactum* may have been a mechanical operation in part, but there is a need to address the question of content as well, since a relationship between model and parody hinges on the recognition of both. Rather than removing form from context, it would be preferable to reconstitute the conditions of contemporary expectation and recognition of liturgical material as a component of troubadour texts. Such recognition would have been a source of initial surprise or polemic, depending on the uses to which parody was put. It is likely that a procession of costumed performers would have displayed similarities to parodic treatments of liturgy, and to the more ludic aspects of rituals associated with the Christmas period.

Reading shared metrical structures can be problematic. Musical structures are neutral, and function as portmanteaux rather than bearers of specific meaning; this tends to lie in the content of the words. For example, Errante's study of the relationship between the Saint Martial song 'De ramis cadunt folia' (MS Paris BN 3719, f. 42r) and Marcabru's *vers* 'Lo vers comens quan vei del fau' (*PC* 293, 33, XXXIII)[20] only considers the shared form. The content of the two songs, with the exception of a shared autumnal opening, is unrelated, which seems to suggest not parody but *contrafactum*. Marcabru's *pastorela* 'L'autrier, a l'issida d'abriu' (*PC* 293, 29, XXIX) shares both its metre and rhyme scheme with a poem from the same codex that is transparently a *canso* in Latin, 'Ecce letantur omnia'.[21] Links between texts involving content and specific images are indications of a more sophisticated level of dialogue that may well be called intertextuality. Margaret Switten's study of the relationship between the sixth-century hymn 'Ave maris stella', the Saint-Martial *versus* 'O Maria Deu maire' and Giraut de Bornelh's *alba* (later rewritten by Cadenet) is a model example of our intertextual dialogue traceable between songs.[22]

Such close dialogue can be traced between another Saint-Martial composition and a troubadour *vers*. The troper Paris BN lat. 3719, signed by Bernard Itier in 1210, features a two-voiced song which is similar in form to the two troubadour texts. The text on f. 19 is the following:

> Homo gaude
> nova laude
> nouum laudans hominem,
> lex nature
> stupet iure
> uirgo parit uirginem.
> Lux caligo
> fit, origo
> finis per originem.

[Man, rejoice! Sing new praises, praising the new man. The law of nature is suspended for sure: a virgin gives birth to a virgin, light becomes darkness, the beginning becomes the end by way of the beginning.]

The song is almost unpunctuated except to demarcate stanzas; the lines are given across the folio.[23] The Marian text is presented in Aquitanian neumes as a piece for two voices, which Spanke and

Blume inferred was a *conductus* on the basis of its closing lines and its two-voiced composition, though sequences were also often polyphonic (*AH*, XX, 124). The partition is heavily melismatic on the b-rhyme, and seems to be divided into four strophes of nine lines, or into three sets of three-line versicles.

That the song may have been the model for Marcabru's *gap* is suggested by its presence in a troper which has already been shown to have been a source for twelfth-century troubadour melodies. It is an extended piece in a single metrical scheme, unlike the isolated stanzas in this metre which exist in Victorine collections. There is a possible parody of this song, or at least of an extended song in this metre, in the Goliardic piece 'Ecce homo sine domo', rubricated *Dictum Goliardi*:

Ecce homo
sine domo,
sine rerum pondere
huc accedit,
quia credit
aliquid accipere.[24]

[Behold the man without a house; without ties, he comes here because he thinks he'll receive something.]

Since the *Analecta Hymnica* feature no songs with the *incipit* 'Ecce homo', it is possible to suppose that this piece is a parody, rather than a *contrafactum*, of a text similar to 'Homo gaude'. 'Ecce homo' is an *unicum* from a fifteenth-century collection (Paris BN nouv. acq. lat. 1544, f. 97^{v}), some items of which may be from the twelfth century. In his edition of the song, Paul Lehmann categorized it as a students' song, written in parody of Pilate's meeting with Christ (John 19:5).[25] Here, the suffering Christ whose cloak is gambled away by soldiers is replaced by a goliard who has gambled away his possessions and is reduced to begging favours from others. Its subject matter points to a connection with parodic gamblers' masses such as the thirteenth-century *Officium lusorum*.[26]

To return to Marcabru's songs: the Saint-Martial-de-Limoges tropers feature a number of hymns to St Andrew (*AH*, VII, n. 121–4, VIII, n. 111). It is likely that there is a parodic relationship between the songs by Marcabru and Peire d'Alvernha and a para-liturgical or liturgical model from Saint-Martial-de-Limoges. While Spanke, Chailley and Errante assumed that the movement of influence was essentially from a Latin model into the vernacular,[27] later scholars have noted that some Latin songs, even early on, have rubrics noting vernacular sources for their melodies.[28] This suggests that influence was a two-way process.

To complicate the picture further, it is important to note that the secular experience of the liturgy before 1215 was probably not extensive, and that people without clerical training may not have had detailed knowledge of the office of the Mass. It is likely, however, that people at court would have had a more frequent experience of the liturgy than those living in an urban or rural environment, but this would not necessarily have been intimate knowledge. The likelihood that the troubadours themselves had often had a clerical education that included training in chant may point to familiarity at least on the part of the poet. Basic literacy may have been more prevalent in Occitan courts than in Northern France, and troubadours display intimate knowledge of moralizing material, proverbs and precepts,[29] but this does not ensure knowledge of Latin, and does not suggest that liturgy would necessarily have been comprehensible to all or most of its congregation. Given such conditions, it is possible to conjecture that passages of chant and of preaching in the vernacular would have been important to the congregation's experience of the Mass, whether 'literate' or not.

The *schola*'s contribution is important to this experience of liturgy and associated rituals. Gregorian chant was embellished and continually developed by a local repertoire of tropes, additions, sequences and *farcitures*. Both manuscript evidence and contemporary sources show that tropes were essentially a monastic genre, often reserved for specific offices, and therefore unlikely to be familiar to anyone not trained in a monastery. However, the *versus* and trope repertoire were also performed on occasion by cathedral choirs, and would have been accessible at such times to a court audience.[30]

The sequence, also known as the *prosa*, was part of the sung liturgy of the Mass, and prominently placed, following on from the *Alleluia*.[31] Its place at the heart of the Mass makes it a genre closer to liturgy than the *versus* and *conductus*, which are generally thought to be occasional and processional pieces.[32] These para-liturgical texts, along with the hymn, have been the focus of much examination of the relationship between liturgy and vernacular lyric, and it is most probable that a troubadour text with parodic reference to the liturgy would contain references to this corpus of chant.[33] There has been some confusion in modern accounts between the sequence and the trope. Whereas the sequence was exclusively performed after the *Alleluia* in the Mass, the trope was a more free-floating element. Saint-Martial-de-Limoges tropers apply the rubric *tropus* to newly composed, neumatic introductions and interpolations in the Proper and Ordinary of the Mass. All essentially literary additions, such as extended codas provided with syllabic texts, either in prose or in poetry, were called *prosae* or *prosulae*. The sequence may initially have consisted of the addition of a text to the extended melisma of the final 'a' of the *Alleluia*. This musical extension, *sequentia*, preceded the Gospel reading and eventually became a distinct and integral musical text.[34]

The same melody could be used for several texts in the *prosae*, whereas the tropes featured newly composed music and words. The *tropus* texts were in prose, with occasional assonance; they had little or no metrical form, and were through-composed, following melodies which were equally free. Finally, the trope flourished between the eleventh and mid-twelfth centuries only, after which it went into a rapid decline, whereas the sequence, in a new form, was the fashionable site for innovation throughout the twelfth century, centring on the Victorine school of composition. By the thirteenth century, the performance of the sequence was well established as a key feature of para-liturgical song, as Gautier de Coincy implies when he exhorts 'clercs et clergesses':

> Chantons, chantons les samedis
> Les déliteuses kyrièles,
> Les séquences plaisans et bèles
> A haute voiz et à haut tons.[35]

Despite its popularity, and the claims made by Pirot, the *versus tripertitus caudatus* was not the norm for the sequence.[36] The corpus of sequences attributed to Adam de Saint-Victor (fl. *c.*1190) in a single manuscript does feature a great many pieces in this form, but they are not representative of one specific period in the twelfth century. Indeed, Victorine sequences have been reinterpreted in recent years as a broader, less standardized corpus.[37] The Victorine sequence may be frequently composed in the 'rime couée', which has the scheme aabccb, but the sequence prior to c.1100 often displayed 'progressive repetition', based on a more or less strict parallelism of versicles, in the sequence aa–bb–cc–dd..., which survived into the twelfth century too.[38] This

'Notkerian' form later developed towards a more strophic form, not unlike the hymn; the date for this shift is now put at the late eleventh or early twelfth century. As a result, it may be possible to conclude that a stanzaic sequence composed in aabccb form around 1100–50 would have been received as relatively innovative. This hypothesis depends initially on a strict definition of the sequence, its history, function and status in the context of twelfth-century liturgical practice.

The early Notkerian sequence was structured as a free set of versicles ordered according to responsion, the repetition of the metrical structure of the first stanza by a 'twin', which is followed by twinned stanzas in different schemes. This responsion structure created the model form aa–bb–cc–dd–...z.[39] The structure is dialogic but paratactic: a series of responding units, isolated from each other. One of the most popular rhymed sequences from the late eleventh century onwards, 'Letabundus', was used as a portmanteau melody and form for at least twenty-six other sequences, as well as other compositions.[40] It is structured in the early style as a set of three-line versicles in parallel pairs:

1a	Letabundus exsultet fidelis chorus, alleluia;	1b	Regem regum intacte profudit thorus, res miranda.
2a	Angelus consilii natus est de virgine, sol de stella.	2b	Sol occasum nesciens, stella semper rutilans, semper clara.

[1a May the faithful choir exult in gladness: Alleluia.
1b The womb of a virgin has borne forth the king of kings: a marvellous event.
2a The angel of counsel is born from a virgin, the sun from a star.
2b A sun which knows no setting, a star that glows for ever, always bright.]

The standardization of the sequence into its Victorine form comes when the parallel versicles become stanzaic, largely by regrouping pairs into blocks. For example, the three-line versicle combines with its responding opposite to create a six-line stanza:[41]

Orbis totus
Unda lotus
Christiani lavavi
Ad Mariam
Matrem piam
Voce clamat alacri.

[The whole Earth, washed by the wave of Christian cleansing, shouts in a glad voice to Mary, the holy mother.]

Stanzas retained a degree of irregularity, however, in that many of the sequences attributed to Adam of Saint-Victor alter stanza and line length throughout. Also, the content of sequences varied considerably, containing elements of hagiography and theology according to context.

It is probably safe to assume that the audience for liturgical sequences in the mid-1130s onwards would have been accustomed to both the old 'free' sequences and the newer, regular, pieces. Its expectation of content would have been wide-ranging, and sometimes dependent on occasion, while an audience in Occitan-speaking regions may have been heavily influenced by the Saint-Martial-de-Limoges repertory. The Limoges abbey owned priories across the whole Southern region, and influenced parts of Northern Spain; Saint Martial-de-Limoges tropes, in Aquitanian notation, are found in manuscripts from this geographical area, whereas the influence of the Northern French repertoire and its notation, from the abbey of Fleury, is slighter.[42] It seems the corpus of liturgical embellishment differed radically between northern and southern regions, with consequent effects on the composition of secular music.

Stevens supposes that the frequency with which one sequence melody is used for a number of others points to the existence of a common fund of tunes for which texts could be created, according to the occasion, and which could be altered to suit the new texts.[43] The Saint-Martial-de-Limoges corpus disseminated a limited number of portmanteau sequence melodies across the Occitan and northern Spanish lands, which would in turn have been open to variation and innovation on a local level. The irregular sequence, for example, survived in the vernacular as the lyric *lai* and *descort* long after it had ceased to be a popular form of new composition.[44]

The positioning of the sequence within the Mass may have made it a focal point for compositions with a message, and the amount of Victorine theology written into the sequences attributed to Adam de Saint-Victor would seem to bear this out.[45] A drunkards' Mass from England places a version of the Archpoet's Confession, 'Estuans intrinsecus', after the Alleluia, in the place of the sequence. Since drunkards' hymns circulated independently in the period, this placing may denote the receptivity of the congregation to a familiar or important song at this moment.[46]

Far from being a stereotyped ecclesiastical genre, the twelfth-century sequence seems in fact to have been a space for stylistic and textual innovation, within the boundaries of its position within the Mass and the liturgical calendar. If the Mass may, as Jacobsson and Treitler have suggested, constitute an overall 'genre', the rubrication or precise definition of the sequence becomes less important than its performance at this particular moment, between the *Alleluia* and the sermon.[47] The sequence offers a wide variety of metrical forms within each piece, of which the 'aabccb' form is only one example, and would have been defined primarily by its positioning and its form, rather than by its content.

As it is, only one troubadour can be proved to have composed both Latin sequences and vernacular poems. The extant corpus of the fourteenth-century troubadour Raimon de Cornet includes two poems in Latin; one is a hymn to the Virgin (Noulet, XVII), and the other a *proza* to St Bernard of Clairvaux (Noulet, XXXIII). The Marian 'canso en lati' is modelled on a vernacular *canso* as six *coblas unissonans* followed by a *tornada*. The *proza* is composed of nine quatrains in the Ambrosian form abba. Raimon de Cornet's Latin songs are extant in a *chansonnier* composed separately from the troubadour tradition, a fact that suggests that other poets may have left similar pieces that were omitted from vernacular anthologies.

Traces of contemporaries' attitudes towards the written texts, and evidence of recognition of liturgical form, may be found to subsist in the *chansonniers*, as evidence that structure was predicated not on the stanza as basic unit, but on either responsion or free patterns of text, preferably based on a three-line aab versicle. This may be taken as a sign of awareness of archaic sequence form, rather than of the *versus*, which was influenced by stanzaic form. For example, Marcabru's *vers* *PC* 293, 33 (Dejeanne, XXXIII) has been likened to a piece from the troper Paris BN lat. 3719, f. 42.[48] Similarly, Marcabru *PC* 293, 9 (IX) and *PC* 293, 6 (VI) are likened to the structure of an Ambrosian hymn. The Ambrosian hymn, which circulated from the seventh century, consisted of eight quatrains of iambic dimeters which eventually became two lines of sixteen syllables each with a marked caesura. The stanzas of the hymn form pairs and are intended for antiphonal performance.[49] This indicates a responsion structure similar to the sequence.

The disparities that emerge in line and stanza length between respective metrical structures were a problem, one later dismissed by

Guido Errante on the grounds that imitation in lyric poetry, being based on melodic structure and an aural dimension, did not entail direct copying.[50] It is also likely that melodies were malleable enough to allow such changes, as has been suggested in a comparison of Jaufre Rudel's 'Lanquan li jorn' with the melody of the hymn 'Ave Regina' in Paris BN lat. 903, f. 162^r.[51] Chambers's comments on the flexibility of formal borrowing in the troubadour lyric must be set against John Marshall's ruling that a significant degree of imprecision should disqualify a song from being termed a *contrafactum*.[52] When similarity of form is sufficiently strong to suggest a similar melody, it may be that there has been borrowing to some extent; the term *contrafactum* should perhaps be reserved for exact replicas, which signal their indebtedness to the model text either in content or in the rubric. It is also worth noting that in the field of *contrafactum* and intertextuality, the margin of error allowing for coincidence can be the site of intense dispute between accident and deliberate allusion. It is possible to read the troubadour corpus as a dense network of interdependent songs, but it is equally possible to suggest that songs addressing a stereotyped fund of themes and images will develop a likeness to each other that may be fortuitous.

Bernadette Masters's work has extended the range of borrowing beyond content and metre, to include aural effect. She assumes that a shared rhythmical, as opposed to metrical, versification may also be traced in related texts.[53] In the early medieval treatises cited by Masters, *rhythmus* is defined as aural scansion, perceived by the ear and the whole body, through performance and beaten time, while *metrum* is perceptible only in written form. This theoretical framework seems to be verified by the parallel French and Latin texts of a sequence to St Eulalia, which share a rhythmical (accentual) structure. Later rhythmic and rhymed Latin pieces often had a complex and shifting melody, which would have obscured the simple metre of the song altogether, a comment also made of the troubadour *vers*.[54] By emphasizing the rhythmical distinctiveness of the verse, at least a trace of the aural shape of a given piece can be preserved.

These issues are important for reading the evidence of shared forms in troubadour poetry. The basic research apparatus for all such studies is István Frank's *Répertoire métrique*, which tabulates the rhyme schemes for all extant poems, and separates each section into subdivisions based on metre. Frank also gives the rhyme sounds of each song, which enables *contrafacta* to be identified with gratifying efficiency. Given the strong rhythm implicit in the 448448 scheme, the shared structures under scrutiny are a combination of rhyme scheme, metre, possibly rhythm and very possibly a shared melody.

Reading Frank's *Répertoire*, it is possible to draw certain conclusions about how generic assumptions influence the choice of metrical scheme. The nine songs in section 193 (aabccb) seem to display a trend away from the *canso*, in that practically all, especially the three in the section with the metre 448448, are either satirical or moralizing. The following items are added in a footnote; these texts are devotional, with the exception of two interrelated songs, often called *ensenhamens*, addressed to *joglars*.

7' 7' 7 7' 7' 7	Anon		prayer to Virgin
	Leys d'Amors, n.26		*cobla* to Virgin
4 4 8 4 4 8	Guerau de Cabrera	*PC* 242a, 1	*ensenhamen* au jongleur
	Guiraut de Calanson	*PC* 243, 7	*ensenhamen* au jongleur
	Peire Cardenal	*PC* 335, 42	sermon

By way of comparison, section 91 (aabaab) features no songs in the 448448 metrical scheme, but has examples of eighteen other forms. This section is, again, not strong on *cansos*; most of the songs are termed *sirventes*. Pirot has pointed out that many of these are aggressive, boastful or mocking, often examples of the *gap* or related types of song. In the form aabaab/888888, two of the songs are by Marcabru and one is by Peire d'Alvernha. The only other example is a *contrafactum* of Peire's song by the Monk of Montaudon.

The *descort* is the troubadour genre most clearly related to the Victorine sequence, and displays the same tendency to regroup several metrical and rhyme schemes within each given song. The term *descort* implies either discord or 'discourtesy', but these songs are only rarely satirical, and hardly ever devotional; they are usually concerned with *canso* thematics. Guiraut de Calanson's *descort* (*PC* 243, 5) has a fifth stanza in which the aab, 448 form is used four times, to produce a twelve-line unit. The examples in Frank are all from the later generation of poets, Guiraut de Calanson, Guillem de la Tor, Cerverí de Girona and Bonifaci Calvo. The most systematic use of the form is found in Cerverí de Girona *PC* 434a, 17, where stanzas 2 to 5, 7, 10, 15, 16 and 18 are in the aabccb form, in the metre 446'446', while stanzas 8, 11 and 13 are in 446'446'6'.[55]

One set of songs, sharing the metrical form 448448, may be isolated from these tables; this subgroup has already been remarked on by several critics over the years. The distinctiveness of their form suggests a common rhythm, and may point to shared melody, though none is extant. Frank shares the uncertainty about the form, suggesting it may be presented as 8888, abcb (Frank, 782a, n.). Chambers and Pirot note the relationships between these songs, all of which are satirical or parodic in some way, and are engaged in dialogue. While Pirot states that they do not share a common model, they do seem to create a network of intertextual allusion, dialogue and copying. They may be regrouped as follows:[56]

(1) A dialogue between Marcabru and Audrics del Vilar, who is likely to be fictive. N'Audric's song 'Tot a estru' (*PC* 16b, 1, Dejeanne, XX) attacks Marcabru, whom he calls 'Pan-Perdut' for being a dissatisfied *joglar*. The reply, 'Senher n'Audric' (*PC* 293, 43, XXb), presents a set of insults to Aldric, renaming him 'Artimalec'.
(2) Marcabru's *vers* 'D'aisso lau Dieu' (*PC* 293, 16, XVI), is parodied, perhaps in his own lifetime, by Peire d'Alvernha in his *vers* 'Be m'es plazen' (*PC* 323, 10, Zenker, XII).
(3) The Catalan troubadour Guerau de Cabrera, who refers to Marcabru in this poem, composes a long poem to a *joglar*, 'Cabra juglar' (*PC* 242a, 1, Pirot, I), listing the skills and texts this performer does not possess. Guerau's poem is copied with certain important differences by Guiraut de Calanson in 'Fadet joglar' (*PC* 243, 7a, Pirot, II), another poem designed to humiliate an ignorant minstrel.
(4) Finally, Peire Cardenal, whose vast corpus of songs is almost exclusively satirical and anticlerical, ends the chain of songs with a versified sermon, 'Predicator' (*PC* 335, 42, Lavaud, LXV).

According to Riquer's datings, the chronology of these compositions is as follows:[57] Marcabru is commonly held to have been active in Poitou and Northern Spain from *c.*1130 to *c.*1150; the *vida*'s claim that Aldrics del Vilar was his initial patron has led to the exchange of songs being placed in the early period, though this is a supposition unsupported by the texts (*BS*, III). Peire d'Alvernha's corpus has been dated through his 'poet's gallery' (*PC* 323, 11)[58] which lists poets active up to around 1170, but omits Marcabru, whom Peire mentions elsewhere as his predecessor and model. His close links to Marcabru's work, for example the parodic relationship between the 'Estornels' songs (dated *c.*1149) and Peire's serious version, may imply that their careers overlapped, perhaps in the early 1150s. He was active in Northern Spain, and is said by his *vida* to have travelled widely (*BS*, XXXIX, 4).

The Catalan troubadour Guerau de Cabrera is a disputed figure. Pirot's study of his poem points out that he is familiar with the 'vers novell' of Jaufre Rudel (fl. *c*.1147) and Marcabru, which would place him among the earliest generations of troubadours, and identifies him as the powerful Catalan nobleman Guerau III de Cabrera (fl. *c*.1130–*c*.1160).[59] However, Stefano Cingolani has suggested a later date for this song, closer to that of Guiraut de Calanson, who was active *c*.1202–*c*.1212, and prefers to identify the author as another Guerau de Cabrera, who was a more prominent patron of the troubadours in Provence and Catalonia in the 1190s. Pirot has dated Guiraut de Calanson's poem *c*.1202.[60]

René Lavaud's datings for Peire Cardenal's songs are often open to doubt, but it is clear that this poet was active in the thirteenth century, in the Auvergne and the Toulousain, and at the court of King Jaime I of Aragon (1213–76); the *vida*'s claim that he lived into extreme old age enables the dating of *c*.1205–*c*.1272 to be accepted (*BS*, L). The versified sermon itself has not been dated, but presents similarities to preaching techniques inspired by the mendicant orders, which would suggest a dating some time after 1215.

This group of songs may be read as a chain of songs that address each other, engaged in a dialogue dependent on their shared form, as well as a concern with the language of authority. The content of the songs seems to be in dialogue, as may be inferred from an adaptation of Gruber's method for identifying intertextual dialogue, the sharing of rhyme-sounds.[61] Peire Cardenal's sermon 'Predicator' also shares a constant b rhyme in *-ar* with Peire d'Alvernha's 'Be m'es plazen' and Marcabru's 'Tot a estru'. While this may be simply an accident resulting from the frequency of *-ar* rhymes in Occitan, there are also shared rhyme words in the three songs. In 'Be m'es plazen', Peire d'Alvernha makes the following statement:

> Qu'ieu ai un cor
>   et un demor
> et un ardit et un pessar,
>   et un amic
>   et un abric
> et a cui me vueill autreiar.
> (stanza 7)

[For I have one heart and one resting-place, and one courage and one concern; and one friend, and one shelter, to whom I wish to give myself.]

The same rhyme words, *cor* and *demor*, occur in 'Predicator':

Ieu ai en cor
Que, per demor,
Ni per rire, ni per jogar,
No.us diga huei
Mal ni enuei
De guiza que.us deia pezar.
(vv. 19–24)

[I have it in mind that, for the sake of laughter, pleasure and play, I should not today say anything negative or unpleasant in such a way as to make you downcast.]

The word *afic* occurs twice in 'Predicator'. It also occurs in Marcabru's song to Aldric, where it indicates obstinacy in making false claims:

Senher N'Aldric
al ver afic
mout etz d'aver secos e plans
(vv. 1–3)

[Sir Audric, with true effort, you say you are very broke.]

The song goes on to allege that Audric's claims to poverty are false, and that he leads a life of luxury and self-indulgence in private. For Peire Cardenal, the obstinacy is that of the would-be preacher, who should be careful to practise what he preaches:

Qui en predic
met son afic
lo fach e.l dich deu ajostar
(vv. 7–9)

[Whoever puts his effort into preaching should make his words conform to his deeds.]

It is also used with reference to the preacher's struggles with his unresponding audience, who do indeed insist on never putting his words into practice:

Con plus vos dic
E plus m'afic
En vos castian enseinhar,
Vos fest pejor
Per c'ai paor
Que m'en covenga a laisar.
(vv. 43–8)

[The more I say to you, the more I persist in teaching you by chastising you, the worse you behave; which is why I'm afraid I might have to give up.]

In Linda Paterson's tabulation of rhymes in the corpus of six troubadours, the *-ic* rhyme, though not particularly rare, appears to be shared by Marcabru and Peire d'Alvernha, and is only used once by Bernart de Ventadorn.[62] Her description of *trobar braus*, 'rough poetry', a style she traces in Marcabru, is one which plays on such hard rhyme sounds in order to express the harsh criticism and chastisement inherent in his moralizing approach. A shared harshness of rhyme sound between Marcabru, Peire d'Alvernha and Peire Cardenal may be related to this cultivation of *castiar*, the term used by Peire in this stanza (though it should be noted that *trobar braus* does not invariably carry satirical elements).

Further links are suggested by Pirot's examination of the relationship betwen Guerau de Carbrera and Marcabru. The *tornada* of 'Hueymais dey esser alegrans' (*PC* 293, 34, XXXIV, vv. 43–9) seems to address Guerau III de Cabrera:

Messatges cortes, ben parlans,
Vai t'en en Urgel ses falhir,
E sias del vers despleyans
A.N Cabrieira, que lo remir,
E potz li dir senes gabar
Qu'en tal loc ai tornat ma sort
On elh poiria pro muzar.

[Courtly, well-speaking messenger, go straight to Urgel, and be the one who unfolds the song before Sir Carbrieira, that he may admire it. And you can tell him, without boasting, that I've turned my fate towards a place where he will only wait in vain.]

This combination of a challenge to a patron, or perhaps a rival, and an allusion to either Crusade or spiritual withdrawal may be linked both to Guerau's song to Cabra, and to Peire d'Alvernha's 'Be m'es plazen'. The statement that he will not boast, followed by a boast, is reminiscent of the *gap*, 'D'aisso lau Dieu'. Guerau's song names Marcabru (vv. 25–30) as one of a group of poets, with Jaufre Rudel; he also refers to a 'n'Arumalec' in v. 200, which is reminiscent of the name Marcabru ascribes to Audric, 'n'Artimalec' in 'Senher N'Aldric', v. 35 (this will be discussed later). Paterson's table shows that the *-ec* rhyme sound is extremely rare, and clearly related, once again, to the *trobar braus*. Furthermore, an insult song addressed by

Lanfranc Cigala to a joglar, 'Lantelm, qui.us onra ni.us acuoill' (*PC* 282, 13, Branciforti, XVII) appears to combine Marcabru's 'Senher N'Audric' with Guerau de Cabrera's 'Cabra juglar':

Qar en perdo
Pren ioglars do
Qe chan renec
 E prec
 E.l dec
 Del bec
Aia d'Artimalec
E.n si descrezensa.
De Carlemaing
O de Galvaing
No saps comtar,
 Siblar,
 Sautar,
 Danzar;
Mas vos sabetz desfar
[Toas] tota covinensa.
 (vv. 53–68)

[For a *joglar* takes a gift in vain who abandons singing, and prays [or pleads], and may he have the commandment of the 'lip' of Artimalec, in such/this unbelief. You can't tell the story of Charlemagne or of Gauvain, nor can you whistle, leap or dance, but you do know how to undo all agreements.]

The passage in Marcabru which this seems to echo is the following:

 De lengueiar
 Contra iocglar
Etz pus afilatz que milas;
 Del vostre bec
 N'Artimalec
No.i iauzira ja crestias.
 (MS *C*, vv. 31–6)

[As regards tongue-wagging against *joglars*, you're sharper than a little hawk; no Christian will ever rejoice in your 'lip', Sir Artimalec.]

The name Artimalec is unstable in manuscripts and has a number of possible associations for its audience, which have been explored by Barbara Spaggiari, who assumes it is derived from the Arabic term *malek*, 'prince', and the prefix *al-*, found in the widespread name 'Abd-el-Malik.[63] A distortion of this name appears to have been used for Saracen characters in Romance texts, such as Ferall Archimalech, a Saracen King of Granada in the *chanson de geste* of *Fierabras*. 'Abd-el-Malik was a relatively common name, and also forms part of the full names of the Hispano-Arabic poets Ibn Quzman (*c.*1086–1160) and Ibn Zuhr (d. *c.*1130). Romance distortion of Arabic names tends to absorb the article and produce one word, so that Ibn Quzman becomes Abencuzmán. The *Ar-* opening of Artimalec would not be typical of such absorptions, which tend to use *A-* or *Al-*.

Moreover, there is no evidence from the text that Artimalec is a Saracen. The text appears to indicate an association with slanderous speech and bad lordship, possibly an allusion to Abimelech (Judges 8:9, 9:5), who is associated typologically with Antichrist in *Bibles moralisées*. As Claudia Panuccio has suggested, however, the best candidate for Marcabru's use of Artimalec is Psalm 51 (*NEB* 52), which opens with the line 'Venit David in domum Achimelech', introducing an invective 'contra calumniatorem praepotentem'. This text includes the accusing lines, 'Tota die iniustitiam cogitavit lingua tua; Sicut novacula acuta fecisti dolum' [forging lies all day against God's loyal servant. Your slanderous tongue is sharp as a razor] (Ps. 51/52: 4).[64] The shared reference to a cutting tongue or mouth, and to aggression against a loyal servant, points to this, not a distortion of Muslim names, being the source of Artimalec.

This does not explain why a similar name occurs in 'Cabra juglar' unless it is associated with a vernacular narrative; perhaps we are dealing with a lost story based on a Biblical tale, but this is only a hypothesis. Aside from this shared name, Guerau's song shares its mode of address, the list in the negative of talents and skills the *joglar* should have, and the list of narratives the *joglar* should perform, concerning Charlemagne (vv. 34–6) and Gauvain (vv. 187–9). Guerau's comment that Cabra cannot sing 'a guiza de juglar guascon' (in the style of a Gascon *joglar*) (v. 12) is echoed in Lanfranc's complaint that Lantelm's audience mistake his 'jangloill' (racket) for a 'chan de Proenza' [Provençal song] (vv. 15–16). Both Lanfranc's and Guerau's songs address questions of repertoire as well as rehearsing the patron–*joglar* exchange format of the exchange between Marcabru and Audric. It is clear that the two sets of pieces are regarded as intertextually bound, and possibly to be performed together. The exchange between Lanfranc Cigala and Lantelm is not included by Witthoeft in his collection of songs he labels *sirventes joglaresc*, and is not examined by Suzanne Thiolier-Méjean in her reconsideration of the corpus. This omission is all the more regrettable, considering the riposte offered by Lantelm.[65]

The dialogue exchange between Marcabru and Audric or Aldrics del Vilar has been analysed several times in proto-biographical terms, based on the statement in one of Marcabru's *vidas* that Aldrics del Vilar was his first patron, at a time in his career when the poet used the name Pan-Perdut (*BS*, IIIB, from *chansonnier A*).[66] In Chambers's reading, the *gap* precedes the exchange between patron and joglar, and illustrates stages in their professional relationship; Spaggiari reads the three songs as a semi-dramatized play, in which Marcabru invites Audric to identify him by adopting an unusual persona in the *gap*, is challenged by Audric to return to his characteristic voice, as 'Pan-Perdut', and obliges his patron with a reply in which he threatens him with a ruined reputation.[67]

Peire Cardenal's sermon is probably the song composed last in the series, and the most distinctive in terms of content. However, while being thematically divorced from the songs addressed to *joglars*, it constructs the speaker as a performer who promises his audience a more entertaining piece after the text in hand. His concern with entertaining his audience with a varied repertoire marks him out as a *joglar*, at least in performance technique, as does his reference to his use of a musical instrument to accompany the next piece, and possibly the present sermon:

> Ar escoutat
> Per eus vos at
> E non vos grev al comensar
> Que a derrier
> D'autre Gautier
> Cug que m'auziretz violar.
> (vv. 13–18)

[Now listen for your own profit, and don't let the opening upset you, for after it, I think you'll hear me play another *gaudeamus* on the *vielle*.]

Lavaud translates the term 'gautier' as a cry: 'Gautier!', on the assumption that the word indicates a refrain or a dance tune. However, the *FEW* notes that the Latin *gaudire* gives rise to a rejoicing song, the *gaudeamus*, which may be secular, and Levy accepts the term in this song as a 'canto de solazzo'. There is also a certain amount of overlap in Old French between *gaudie*, meaning joy or frolic, and *godie*, mockery, while Greimas mentions the *gaudin*, a thirteenth-century term for a 'chanson commençant par un *gaudeamus*'.[68] It seems more appropriate, therefore, to translate the term here as a *gaudeamus*: a rejoicing song with spiritual overtones, akin to the chant 'Gaudeamus igitur'.

While this passage may refer to the preacher changing his tune metaphorically, from criticism to exhortation, it also indicates a context of performance in which audience reaction is essential. In the manuscripts, 'Predicator' is indeed followed by Peire Cardenal's collected *sirventes*. Guerau de Cabrera's song uses the same rhyme word, *viular*, to refer to the skills of a secular performer:

Mal saps viular
e pietz chantar
del cap tro en la fenizon;
non saps fenir
al mieu albir
a tempradura de breton.
(vv. 7–12)

[You play the *vielle* badly, you sing worse, from top to the end [of a song]; in my opinion, you can't finish [a melody] in Breton style.]

This reference to a combination of *vielle* and song would seem to confirm that, contrary to the received opinion that troubadour 'high style' songs were sung *a capella*, the *vielle* was an intrinsic part of performance.[69]

Guerau de Cabrera's song is copied by Guiraut de Calanson in 'Fadet juglar', a *contrafactum* which enters into competitive dialogue with its model. As a commentary by an imperfect poet on Guerau's reverse boast (he notes he has forgotten half of his model, vv. 7–12), Guiraut's poem reverses the negative description, changing it into a prescriptive list of skills and texts. Rather than attacking the *joglar* for the knowledge he lacks, Guiraut's song lists those things he should learn: 'Sapchas trobar/ e gen tombar/ e ben parlar, e jocs partir' (You should know how to compose, how to tumble nicely, how to speak well, and to debate poetry) (vv. 13–15).

The intertextual evidence would appear to be in favour of treating Marcabru's three songs as close textual relations of Peire d'Alvernha's 'Be m'es plazen' and Guerau de Cabrera's 'Cabra juglar'. In turn, the texts beget secondary offspring, in the shape of Guiraut de Calanson's 'Fadet juglar' and the exchange between Lanfranc Cigala and Lantelm, as well as Peire Cardenal's sermon, 'Predicator', which has reminiscences of several members of the series. Marcabru's 'D'aisso lau Dieu' has intertextual links both with Guiraut de Calanson's 'Fadet juglar' in the lines 'e savis si gart al partir' (Marcabru, v. 27) and 'can ve al partir' (Guiraut, v. 222), and with Peire Cardenal's 'Predicator' in the parallel closures 'Cascun si gart' (Marcabru, v. 55) and 'Per so dic que chascus se gar' (Peire, v. 186). The songs are all associated with issues of performance, boasting, skill and authority, either in performance or in naming; ultimately, all the songs in the series are bound up with a discussion of knowledge.

The copying of Marcabru's formal devices, vocabulary and style involves a participation in a debate over the exploitation of form, as well as an entrance into a 'lineage' of textual descendants.[70] By extending this series of parodies to include Guilhem IX's songs, as well as evidence that the form is associated with didactic texts, the field of parody becomes extensive, and the initial hypotexts are locatable. The intertextual 'family' thus established features songs which fit only marginally into the definition of lyric poetry, but are all included in the *chansonniers*.

Form and layout are crucial to this intertextual dialogue. All have been edited by various scholars in six-line stanzas, often with oscillation between shorter, three-line units for longer pieces, and the use of a nine-line stanza for shorter songs. For example, while Rita Lejeune proposes that 'Cabra juglar' is accessible only through a stanzaic format, as opposed to the more discursive sermon 'Predicator', Frank Chambers takes a different view, preferring a stanzaic format for the sermon, and the contrary for 'Cabra juglar'.[71] It is important to examine the evidence of scribal practice, to see if anything can be established about the form that was applied to these texts.

Notes to Chapter 2

1. Aurelio Roncaglia, 'Il *gap* di Marcabruno', *Studi Medievali* 17 (1951), 46–70 (47).
2. Roncaglia, 'Il *gap* di Marcabruno', 62, citing from Paul Meyer's edition, 'Anciennes poésies religieuses en langue d'Oc', *Bibliothèque de l'Ecole des Chartes* 5/1 (1860), 481–97.
3. Meyer, 'Anciennes poésies religieuses', 481.
4. François Pirot, *Recherches sur les connaissances littéraires des troubadours occitans et catalans des XIIe et XIIIe siècle: les 'sirventes ensenhamens' de Guerau de Cabrera, Guiraut de Calanson et Bertrand de Paris* (Barcelona: Real Academía de Buenas Letras, 1972), 96–105 (100).

5. Maria Luisa Meneghetti, 'Un stornello nunziante. Fonti, significato e datazione dei due *vers* dell'estornel di Marcabru', *Cantarem d'aquestz trobadors: Studi occitanici in onore di Giuseppe Tavani*, ed. Luciano Rossi (Alessandria: Edizioni dell'Orso, 1995), 47–63. The connection with a *muwashshah* by Al-Abyad was first made by A. R. Nykl, *Hispano-Arabic Poetry and its Relations with the Old Provençal Troubadours* (Baltimore: J. H. Furst, 1946), 245–6.
6. Jean Beck, *La Musique des troubadours* (Paris: Stock, 1979), 30–1.
7. Nicolò Pasero, 'Pastora contro cavaliere, Marcabruno contro Guglielmo IX: Fenomeni di intertestualità in "L'autrier jost' una sebissa"', *Cultura Neolatina* 43 (1983), 9–25.
8. See Hans Spanke, *Untersuchungen über die Ursprünge des romanischen Minnesangs: Marcabrustudien* (Göttingen: Vandenhoek und Ruprecht, 1940), 14–15.
9. Maria Domenica Legge, *Anglo-Norman Literature and its Background* (Oxford: Oxford University Press, 1963), 180–1; *Anglo-Norman in the Cloisters* (Edinburgh: Edinburgh University Press, 1950), 13–17; 'La Versification anglo-normande au XIIe siècle', *Mélanges offerts à René Crozet*, ed. Pierre Gallais and Jean-Yves Riou, 2 vols. (Poitiers: Centre d'Etudes Médiévales, 1966), i. 639–43.
10. Monson, *Les 'Ensenhamens' occitans*, 157–8.
11. Suzanne Thiolier-Méjean, 'De la rupture comme principe esthétique du *sirventes*', in *Studia occitanica in memoriam Paul Rémy*, ed. Hand-Erich Keller, 2 vols. (Kalamazoo: Medieval Institute Publications, 1986), ii. 313–22. See also *La Poétique des troubadours: trois études sur le sirventés* (Paris: Presses de l'Université de Paris-Sorbonne, 1994), 206–32.
12. Goddard, 'The Early Troubadours', 18–23.
13. Kendrick, *Game of Love*, 15–23; Martindale, 'Cavalleria et orgueil'.
14. Camille, *The Medieval Art of Love* (London: Laurence King, 1998), 119.
15. Dronke, *Medieval Latin Poetry*, 287.
16. Misset and Aubry (eds.), *Proses d'Adam de Saint Victor*, 40.
17. Stevens, *Words and Music*, 324–30.
18. Karl Young, *The Drama of the Medieval Church*, 2 vols. (Oxford: Clarendon Press, 1933), ii. 125–71, text: 138–44; Lynette Muir, *The Biblical Drama of Medieval Europe* (Cambridge: Cambridge University Press, 1995), 83–5, 204 n.
19. Stevens, *Words and Music*, 327.
20. Guido Errante, *Marcabru e li fonte sacre dell'antica lirica romanza* (Florence: Sansoni, 1948), 140.
21. Dronke, *Medieval Latin Poetry*, 293, 380–2.
22. Switten, 'Modèle et variations'.
23. *AH*, XX, n. 159. Hans Spanke, 'St-Martial Studien. Ein Beitrag zur frühromanischen Metrik', *Zeitschrift für französische Sprache und Literatur* 54 (1930–1) 282–317, 385–422, 309; Dronke, *The Medieval Lyric*, 39.
24. Lehmann, *Die Parodie im Mittelalter*, 151–2.
25. Lehmann, *Die Parodie im Mittelalter*, 208–9.
26. Bayless, *Parody in the Middle Ages*, 98–119.
27. Hans Spanke, *Beziehungen zwischen romanischer und mittellateinischer Lyrik* (Göttingen: Vandenhoek und Ruprecht, 1936); Chailley, 'Les premiers troubadours et les *versus* de l'école d'Aquitaine', *Romania* 76 (1955), 212–35; Errante, *Marcabru*, 90–104.

28. Dronke, *Medieval Lyric*, 39–40.
29. Wendy Pfeffer, *Proverbs in Medieval Occitan Literature* (Gainesville: University of Florida Press, 1997).
30. Chailley, *L'Ecole musicale*, 43, 46.
31. See Nancy Van Deusen, 'Polymelodic sequences and a "second epoch" of sequence composition', in *Musicologie médiévale: Notations et séquences*, ed. Michel Huglo (Paris: Champion, 1987), 213–25 (218); Gerhard Podhrasky, *New Dictionary of the Liturgy*, ed. and trans. Lancelot Sheppard (London: Geoffrey Chapman, 1967), 183. See also Stevens, *Words and Music*, 80–109.
32. See Chailley, 'Premiers troubadours' and *L'Ecole musicale*, 213–74, as well as Diehl, *Religious Lyric*, 90–1, and David Hughes, 'Music and meter in liturgical poetry', *Medievalia et Humanistica* 7 (1976), 29–49 (33).
33. Bernadette Masters, *Esthétique et manuscripture: le 'moulin à paroles' au Moyen Age* (Heidelberg: Winter, 1992), 223–32.
34. Paul Evans, *The Early Trope Repertory of Saint Martial de Limoges* (Princeton: Princeton University Press, 1970), 3–17; André Madrignac and Danièle Pistone, *Le Chant Grégorien: historique et pratique* (Paris: Champion, 1981), 42–4; Misset and Aubry (eds.), *Proses d'Adam*, 46; Eugenio Costa, *Tropes et séquences dans le cadre de la vie liturgique au Moyen Age* (Rome: C.L.V. Edizioni liturgiche, 1979), 8–15; Masters, *Esthétique et manuscripture*, 223–4.
35. Young, *Drama of the Medieval Church*, i. 194–5.
36. Pirot, *Recherches*, 100.
37. MS Paris BN lat. 14452, in *Proses d'Adam*, ed. Misset and Aubry; Margot Fassler, 'Who was Adam de Saint-Victor?', *JAMS* 37 (1984) 233–69; Meneghetti, 'Un stornello nunziante', *Studi Tavani*, 57.
38. Stevens, *Words and Music*, 82.
39. Stevens, *Words and Music*, 82–109; Lars Elfving, *Etude lexicographique sur les séquences limousines* (Stockholm: Almqvist & Wiksell, 1962), 8, 258.
40. Text from Stevens, *Words and Music*, 91–8, 91, n. 23.
41. See Stevens, *Words and Music*, 104, for a discussion of the dating; Wrangham (ed.), *Adam*, iii. 118, n. xciv.
42. Chailley, *L'Ecole musicale*, 26, 48.
43. Stevens, *Words and Music*, 105–9, and Evans, *Early Trope Repertoire*, 11–13.
44. Stevens, *Words and Music*, 110–55.
45. Misset and Aubry (eds.), *Proses d'Adam*, 57–65.
46. Bayless, *Parody in the Middle Ages*, 105–9.
47. Ritva Jacobsson and Leo Treitler, 'Tropes and the Concept of Genre', in *Pax et Sapientia: Studies in Text and Music of Liturgical Tropes and Sequences*, ed. Ritva Jacobsson (Stockholm: Almqvist & Wiksell, 1986), 87.
48. Spanke, *Beziehungen*, 116.
49. Diehl, *Religious Lyric*, 37–8, 76–8.
50. Errante, *Marcabru*, 79.
51. Hendrik Van der Werf, *Extant Troubadour Melodies: Transcriptions and Essays for Performers and Scholars* (Rochester, NY: The Author, 1984), 73–5.
52. Chambers, 'Imitation of Form in the Old Provençal Lyric', and John Marshall, 'Pour l'étude des *contrafacta* dans la poésie des troubadours', *Romania* 101 (1980) 289–335 (290).

53. Masters, *Esthétique et manuscripture*, 189–204, 223–34.
54. Hughes, 'Music and Metre', 31; Diehl, *Religious Lyric*, 89.
55. Frank, *Répertoire métrique*, i. pp. xl-xlii.
56. Frank M. Chambers, *Introduction to Old Provençal Versification* (Philadelphia: American Philosophical Society, 1985), 267–71; id., 'D'Aisso lau Dieu and Aldric del Vilar', *Romance Philology* 35 (1981–2), 489–500; Pirot, *Recherches*, 103–4, n. 37.
57. de Riquer, *Los Trovadores*, i. 170–2, 311–12.
58. For a new edition and interpretation of this song, see Luciano Rossi, 'Per l'interpretazione di '*Cantarai d'aquests trobadors* (323, 11)', in *'Cantarem d'aquestz trobador': Studi occitanici in onore di Giuseppe Tavani*, ed. Luciano Rossi (Alessandria: Edizioni dell'Orso, 1995), 65–111.
59. Pirot, *Recherches*, 17–73; Stefano Cingolani, 'Le *sirventes-ensenhamen* of Guerau de Cabrera: A proposal for a new interpretation', *Journal of Hispanic Research* 1 (1992–3), 191–200.
60. Pirot, *Recherches*, 192–6, 256–61.
61. Gruber, *Dialektik des Trobar.*
62. Linda Paterson, *Troubadours and Eloquence* (Oxford: Oxford University Press, 1975), 215–22; Marcabru *PC* 293, 22, 26, 32, XXII, XXVI, XXXII; Peire d'Alvernha *PC* 323, 24, XI; Raimbaut d'Aurenga, *PC* 389, 24, Pattison, XVII; Bernart de Ventadorn, *PC* 70, 24, XXIV; also ibid. 217–20.
63. Barbara Spaggiari, 'Artimalec e *Archimalec*', *Romania* 111 (1990), 331–45, 338–9; Nykl, *Hispano-Arabic Poetry*, 266, 247–9.
64. Claudia Panuccio, review of Spaggiari, *Il Nome di Marcabru*, in *Medioevo Romanzo* 19 (1994), 195–200, 199, n. 4. See also Gianfranco Contini, 'A propos de *tribu martel*', *Romania* 63 (1937), 253–66, and Richard Emmerson, *Antichrist in the Middle Ages: A Study of Medieval Art, Apocalypticism and Literature* (Seattle: University of Washington Press, 1981).
65. Friedrich Witthoeft, *Sirventes Joglaresc* (Marburg: Elwert, 1891); Suzanne Méjean, 'Contribution à l'étude du *sirventes joglaresc*', *Mélanges de philologie romane dédiées à la mémoire de Jean Boutière,* ed. I. Cluzel and F. Pirot, 2 vols. (Liège: Solédi, 1971), i. 377–95. See my article, 'Negative Self-Promotion: The troubadour *sirventes joglaresc*', in *The Court and Cultural Diversity: Selected Papers from the Eighth Triennial Congress of the ICLS, The Queen's University of Belfast, 26 July–1 August, 1995*, ed. Evelyn Mullally and John Thompson (Woodbridge: D. S. Brewer, 1997), 47–56.
66. Jean-Charles Huchet, *Littérature médiévale et psychanalyse* (Paris: Presses Universitaires de France, 1990); Chambers, 'D'Aisso lau Dieu and Aldric del Vilar'; Barbara Spaggiari, *Il nome di Marcabru: Contributi di onomastica e critica testuale* (Spoleto: Centro italiano di studi sull'alto medioevo, 1992).
67. Chambers, 'D'Aisso lau Dieu and Aldric del Vilar'; Spaggiari, *Il nome di Marcabru*, 45–52.
68. Lavaud, *Peire Cardenal*, 427 n.; *FEW*, iv. 75–82; *PSW*, iv. 88. A.-J. Greimas, *Dictionnaire de l'ancien français* (Paris: Larousse, 1980), 310.
69. Joel Cohen, 'Peirol's Vielle: Instrumental Participation in the Trobador Repertory', *Historical Performance* 3/2 (1990), 73–7, but see Christopher Page, *Voice and Instruments in the Middle Ages: Instrumental Practice and Songs in France, 1100–1300* (London: Dent, 1987), 29–33; de Riquer, *Los Trovadores*, ii. 1113.

70. Roncaglia, 'Lo *gap* di Marcabru', 65, 70; Amelia Van Vleck, *Memory and Recreation in Troubadour Lyric* (Berkeley: University of California Press, 1991),
71. Rita Lejeune, 'La forme de *l'ensenhamen au jongleur* du troubadour Guiraut de Cabrera', *Estudis Romànics* 9 (1961), 171–81 (172–4, 181); Chambers, 'D'Aisso lau Dieu'.

CHAPTER 3

❖

Recognition and Recollection of Form and Content

Scribal recognition of a distinctive metrical structure is a thorny issue in vernacular as well as in Latin songs. The verse-form aab/448 fits Jeanroy's account of the disintegration of the Classical Latin trochaic tetrameter into three separate lines,[1] a development which, he states, scribes chose to represent in a variety of ways. Modern editors have hesitated between strophic, versicle-parallel and continuous verse patterns when dealing with this corpus of songs, with varying results. Pirot's decision to edit the *sirventes* of Guerau de Cabrera in six-line stanzas disqualifies it from being categorized as a sequence-related form in three-line parallel versicles; this is based on Lejeune's decision that the content of the *sirventes* by Guerau de Cabrera indicates a division into stanzas, whereas Bartsch's edition of 1856 had presented 'Cabra juglar' as a long chain of three-line versicles.[2] Given François Zufferey's point that reading a given scribe's text for its individual system depends on awareness of the spatial dimensions chosen for the song, it is worth examining the scribal choices exercised for the corpus of troubadour songs under scrutiny here, in order to establish if there is any hesitation, in terms of format, rubric or classification, between stanzaic or sequential form.[3]

Far from being 'mere' punctuation, the use of end-stops and the indication of breaks between stanzas were both crucial elements in the compilation of texts, as well as in medieval mnemonics. In this context, the transcription of a song entailed both reading and memorization, the 'sound' of a text being inscribed in the shape it took on the page. As Leo Treitler has pointed out, performance and inscription of a song both involve remembering *and* composing, without necessarily referring to a written source.[4] Mary Carruthers's powerful examination of treatises on memory shows that the reader was enjoined to impress on his memory the layout, colour, shape and punctuation of the source, all the better to recollect it:

Therefore it is of great value for fixing a memory-image that when we read books, we study to impress on our memory [...] not only the number and order of verses or ideas, but at the same time the colour, shape, position and placement of the letters [...] in what location (at the top, the middle or the bottom) we saw it positioned, in what colour we observed the trace of the letter or the ornamented surface of the parchment.[5]

This was considered important to the point of insisting that the same manuscript should be consulted every time, to avoid muddying the memorizing process. Concern over punctuation was bound up with the imperative that the accurate placing of a *cola* [stop] was crucial to the very process of reading.[6] The signs marking the physical appearance of the text for both reading and recollection were as important as musical notation was to a singer.[7] Such ideas about punctuation imply that the placing of end-stops was not an inadequate sign-system to be corrected by those in possession of more advanced technology, but a key element in the transmission and reception of troubadour texts. If a scribe seems to have punctuated a song in a form that reflects a non-stanzaic formal assumption, this may be evidence that the song was not understood to be stanzaic. This consideration casts new light on the question of *mouvance*; if troubadour songs seem to have been transmitted both accurately and with considerable permutation in stanza order, this may be related to the role of memorization in the written as well as the oral process of transmission.

The presentation of melodies with texts in *chansonniers* and tropers is quite dissimilar. Later Saint-Martial-de-Limoges tropers contain less musical notation than might be expected, which makes them compatible with the *chansonniers*' paucity in terms of written melodies, but musical notation in the *chansonniers* follows a distinctive approach that occasionally points to an uncertain grasp of Gregorian chant systems. The Occitan melodic corpus is extant only in four manuscripts, the Occitan *R* and *G* and Old French *W* and *X*. In his edition of these pieces, Hendrik Van der Werf notes that *R*, in particular, verges on incoherence, which he explains as the work of a scribe who was incompletely trained in Gregorian notation.[8] It may be argued that the scribes collating vernacular melodies either were out of practice, or encountered difficulties adapting the Latin system, which was modal and melismatic, to an isosyllabic scheme, in which one note corresponded to one syllable of text.

However, the isosyllabic hypothesis has been questioned with reference to Anglo-Norman verse by Bernadette Masters, who points out that shared melodies do give rise to shared systems of notation.[9] Masters's thesis is that Anglo-Norman versification is influenced by Old English pronunciation and stress systems, and therefore differs from the Old French metrical forms, which it does not corrupt but alters, by being accentual and rhythmic. This may be applied, in turn, to Occitan versification; Vincent Pollina has suggested that Occitan, as an accentuated language, requires a compromise between strict isosyllabic metre and stress patterns emerging from the spoken words.[10] The fact that Anglo-Norman and Occitan versification include the *versus tripertitus caudatus* suggests that the hesitations over form in the two fields may be compatible. There seem to be grounds for supposing that editorial vacillations reflect not modern perceptions but an uncertainty about form, understood in terms of versification and genre, among the compilers of the *chansonniers*.

The layout and rubrics of the manuscripts reflect scribal indecision about metrical structure, for example in Peire Cardenal's sermon 'Predicator' as opposed to Marcabru's *vers* 'D'aisso lau Deu'. This brings into question how conventionalized the lyric pieces in the corpus were for the scribes. The same question may be asked of the two *sirventes* of Guerau de Cabrera and Giraut de Calanson.

Peire Cardenal's sermon is extant in manuscripts *IKTDa*. It appears twice in *K*, an example of scribal hesitation about positioning as well as form which is worthy of note, considering the 'dissimilar twin' status of *IK*. *IK* open their *sirventes* section with Peire Cardenal's *sirventes* and sermons, an interesting move, since they place Cercamon and Marcabru at the start of the *canso* section. This may be a result of the *chansonniers*' historicization of the troubadour corpus, which leads them to categorize all songs, regardless of content, from the period when they were known as *vers* to the *canso* section, and to treat the *sirventes* of Bertran de Born and Peire Cardenal as a separate genre.[11]

In *I*, the text is rubricated as 'peire cardinal sermons' and separated into stanzas by a swirl of alternating colour. In troubadour *chansonniers*, line endings are marked by line stops, a single dot, within continuous columns of text. If the line stops are assumed to signal the metrical scheme of the song, Peire Cardenal's text is envisaged as a stanzaic piece, in four octosyllabic units:

Predicator tenc per meillor
cant fai l'obra que manda far.
no fas sellui qui l'obra fui
e als autres vai predicar.

This seems to shift the form from an aabccb lyric stanza into an octosyllabic, four-line unit with internal rhyme and a caesura; this is found in Anglo-Norman versified sermons, histories and chronicles composed in the twelfth century.[12] This is also associated with the *strophe couée*, or tail-rhyme stanza, but one which is not so much lyric as associated with narrative and with versified sermons. It appears, however, to be an imperfect way of presenting this piece; it is, in fact, probably a telling misrecognition on the part of the scribe, based on generic rather than formal assumption, as the two versions in *K* seem to bear out.

The *K* texts show the scribal problem in hand; *K* has two versions of 'Predicator', a fragment on f. xi (*K1*) and the full text in the *sirventes* section f. 159^r (*K2*). While this is evidence of a basic compiler's mistake in misplacing the text, the initial fragment is not identical with the full version. In *K1*, the index of *incipit* lines for the *sirventes* section is followed by two blank folios, after which the Peire Cardenal section seems to open. Peire's *vida* is followed by the rubric 'peire cardinals sermons', the text of 'Jhesus Crist' and the opening of 'Predicator', as in the full version. The large spaces for the capital letters P and J have been left unfilled, and the folio appears to have been abandoned at a first stage of transcription of the finished texts. The format for both sermons is a continuous block, with no signs for divisions into stanzas, though it is clearly meant to be verse.

'Predicator' is abandoned at line 32, though it is only on the first column of the folio. Despite the lack of stanza divisions on the folio, *K*1 may intend a stanzaic format, since perceptible gaps have been made in the text between specific lines. There is what seems to be a false start; the scribe opens with a four-line stanza, then goes on to a second stanza presented as six lines. The scribe starts with a continuous piece in mind, begins to discern a stanzaic, six-line format, and abandons the attempt at transcription. The full version, *K*2, starts with stanza divisions identical to *I*, then moves on to a six-line format, from which it rarely swerves. It starts a new stanza on a new line, a much clearer statement about structure, and one which brings it closer to the lyric. The text, as a result, appears to be more assured about its form: it is opened with a preface of four octosyllabic lines, and continued in regular stanzas. Interestingly, the hymn to the Virgin edited by Meyer and cited by Roncaglia as the model for the aabccb form of Marcabru's *gap* also opens with a four-line preface, in alexandrines, before a long section of hexasyllables.

Manuscript *T* presents a different problem. The Peire Cardenal section is from a different source to the rest of the *chansonnier*, and 'Predicator' (f. 91^{v}) is compiled after the sermon 'Jhesus Crist' (*PC* 335, 27, LV) and the *faula* 'Una ciutat fo' (Lavaud, LXXX). 'Predicator' and 'Una ciutat fo' are treated as continuous pieces; each line is separate, beginning at the margin, and there is no punctuation, save a capital letter at the start of the *faula*'s moral. The texts are not rubricated, and are unsigned. 'Jhesus Crist', on the other hand, adopts a different style, and comprises similar stanza divisions to the main text of 'Predicator' in *IK*, but in a pattern that seems disorganized, until the text returns to a format of continuous lines. Furthermore, the transition to 'Predicator' here has no rubric and is not clearly defined, which suggests an imperfect source that may have been common to *IKT*. 'Una ciutat fo' is a piece composed in four-line octosyllables, aabb, and rubricated in *I* as 'sermons VII', which leads Lavaud to ask if this indicates that Peire originally composed seven didactic or narrative texts, of which only three survive in the *chansonniers*.[13] The text of 'Predicator' in *T* is given in a continuous block undivided by stanzas, but with line stops provided:

> Predicators.
> tenc per meillors   qua fa aco que manda far
> Non fas selui.
> qui l'obra fui   que als autres vai prezicar
> Qui son afic.
> met en prezicz   los fach e.ls dichs deu aiostar

This incoherent system of two-line segments breaks down in one line into 6:2: 'Car mieils lo cre aquel . qe.l ve'. Interestingly, the following piece is the *sirventes* 'Ab votz d'angel' (*PC* 335, 1, XXVIII), which is presented in the classic lyric stanzaic format, with a capital letter indicating each new stanza, though there is a certain amount of hesitation by the scribe as to whether to adopt a stanzaic block or a line-by-line format. Despite this uncertainty, the song is more clearly inscribed as a lyric piece than the sermon, since it is allotted clear stanzaic units. In *T*, 'Predicator' is written as a set of three-line units, and not considered to be a lyric poem.

Manuscript *Db* contains a single-author collection for Peire Cardenal. The text of 'Predicator' (f. 241), unrubricated, is interspersed with diagonal dashes above the text, which seems to be intended as a continuous octosyllabic monologue. The dashes may be indications of accentuation or rhythm, but are not regular. The poem is divided into twelve-line stanzas, with a large capital letter marking these intervals; lines are provided with line stops, which makes them all the more definite.

There is no rubric and no perceptible break between the end of this piece and the opening of the following, the *cobla esparsa* 'Tostemps volgra.m vengues bonaventura' (*PC* 335, 59, XC) which, in turn, runs into the song after it. This implies a jumbled source, which left the scribe unable to distinguish between individual texts, let alone genres. The careful annotations and layout of 'Predicator', however, suggest a performer's copy, and the *joglar*-preacher's promise of another *gautier* afterwards may explain the abrupt transition to a short piece celebrating wealthy patrons and sincere friendship.

These four manuscripts show waverings about format which prompt those of modern editors. All five versions discussed above treat 'Predicator' as a generic exception to the lyric corpus, either in its format or in its rubrication, although the *K* index does not distinguish *sermons* from *sirventes*.

The formats for 'Predicator' are similar to those adopted in other versified sermons from the Old French and Anglo-Norman French corpus, in the *strophe couée*. Suchier's edition of the two sermons, including 'Grant mal fist Adam', opts for a six-line stanza format:

> Grant mal fist Adam
> quant por le Sathan
> entamat le fruit.
> Mal conseil [li] don
> qu'iceo li loat
> car tost l'out sozduit.[14]

Tanquerey does likewise in his edition of a *sermon en vers*, the 'Roman des Romans'.[15] Neither editor specifies the format chosen by the scribes in their base texts. Manuscript B of Suchier's edition of 'Grant mal fist Adam' is part of a thirteenth-century English volume, compiled in an Augustinian monastery, Gonville and Caius MS 435, ff. 129–35. It is probable that this sermon, given its context, is intended for penitential occasions. Its format is not six-line stanzas, but continuous lines of roughly fifteen syllables each:

> Grant mal fist Adam ki par le satan tel conseil crut.
> mal conseil li duna qi ce lui lea car tost lot sesduit.

The layout emphasizes separate lines, to the extent of filling in incomplete spaces with a line of red ink; there are line stops, but not for each line. There is, therefore, no indication of a stanzaic structure, and the verse is transcribed as a version of the trochaic tetrameter, with internal rhymes, in lines of between thirteen and fifteen syllables each:

> Grant mal fist Adam   ki par le Satan   tel conseil crut.

Similarly, Stengel's edition of three Anglo-Norman versions of the *Disticha Catonis* uses the *strophe couée*, but only throughout the text of one, the version attributed to 'Averard le moine'.[16] The texts by Elie de Wincestre and the Anonymous are in octosyllables, which suggests an oscillation similar to that of the Occitan texts above.

It would be possible to conclude on the basis of these examples that the aabccb metrical structure is a source of confusion for many scribes. What this form would have meant in performance raises the question of whether a versified sermon was sung, declaimed or read aloud. Given assertions about the irregularity of melodies associated with regular formal structures in songs, it is likely that performance would have obscured the matter of audible pauses between lines or stanzas, increasing hesitation for scribes.

By way of contrast, *IK* and *T* allot Marcabru's three songs in 448448, aabccb a six-line stanzaic form, signalling stanza breaks by colour change for the first letter in *I* (f. 118^{v}). The format appears to be accepted without demur, though the *I* version of 'Senhers N'Audric' has a first stanza combined with the last of 'Tot a estru' into a twelve-line block, and the line 'vos faill la carns e.l vins e.l pans' is divided by a line stop into two four-syllable sections. *Chansonnier C*, on the other hand, appends three additional versicles onto the third stanza of 'Senher N'Audric', making it nine lines long, and at the end splits the final stanza into two separate sets of three-line versicles. For the scribe of *C*, therefore, the basic unit is a three-line versicle, not the six-line stanza.

Da (f. 208^{r}) presents the exchange between Marcabru and Audric in one complete block separated neither by a rubric nor by a space, but adopts a different format for the two songs. Audric addresses Pan-Perdut/Marcabru in six-line stanzas, but the reply is structured in nine-line units:

Seigner N'Oldric
al vostr'afic
es ben d'aver socons e plans
pos ço disez
et es non avez
q'en setenbre vos faill lo grans
lai us nadau
sai autrestau
qe vo faill charnz e vins e pans

Since this exchange is attributed to Ugo Catola, it is likely to be from a faulty source, but this does not detract from the fact that *I*, *C* and *Da* seem to consider the three-line unit to be the basic format of these stanzaic songs. As far as these scribes are concerned, the three-line versicle in aab competes with the stanza as the core unit of these songs.

The case of Guerau de Cabrera's song is interesting in this respect. *Da* places it before Giraut de Calanson's parody, in which the successor states that his model was written down but that he is working from an imperfectly memorized version (*Da* f. 204^{r}). 'Cabra juglar' and 'Fadet juglar' are intended for public performance in terms of their direct address to a silent *joglar*; it is likely that Giraut's complaint about his memory is a means of justifying the piece's composition, as well as a joke about Guerau's criticism of Cabra's inadequate memory. This implies that Guerau's text circulated in writing, which has implications for the format chosen on the folio in the *chansonnier*, which claims to be a copy of the earliest known collection of troubadour songs, the *Liber Alberici*, dated 1254.[17] If the dating in terms of the content of the song, to *c.*1147, is accurate, this would imply that Guerau's song was transmitted for over a century before transcription in the source for *Da*. However, Giraut de Calanson's poem is from the *c.*1190–6 period; it is possible to surmise that Giraut's written source may be a version fifty years junior to the composition of the original piece.[18] In this piece, written form seems to provide a further comment on content. Giraut de Calanson's text is a *contrafactum* of a preceding parodic text which opened with an enumeration of lyric genres; Guerau de Cabrera's text is a list of narratives from a wide variety of traditions, and this is replicated, but with a stronger emphasis on performance, by his successor.

It would appear that there is some awareness of a basic liturgical model, based on parallelism, response and three-line versicle structure. The pieces in the corpus established here appear to be intended for performance accompanied by a musical instrument, most probably the *vielle* to which two refer, and for a sung or declaimed delivery. This is explained by the specific method of composition for the *vers*, which favoured rhapsodic, through-composed melodies; such a theory would appear to go against the driving rhythm and simple melodic lines suggested by the metrical structure 448448, aabccb/aab. While the sermon and the two long addresses to a *joglar* are preserved in lyric manuscripts, they are not widely disseminated, and the sermons are allotted special status in Peire Cardenal's corpus. Marcabru's and Peire d'Alvernha's songs, however, are included in the lyric repertoire without evidence that transmission was affected by their form, but the three-line versicle as a basic organizing factor is clearly present in the background of their transcription as isostrophic texts.

It is important to note that this series of songs forms a small and specific group within the surviving subgroup of troubadour songs in the form aabccb/aab. Some are treated as lyric pieces, while others are hybrids, combining narrative and didactic genres. In general, all are texts which play on aggression or didacticism, and none are concerned with the love lyric. Their form provides them with a driving rhythm, and they were destined for sung performance as entertainment; indications of dialogue and enactment within or between them point to performed cycles. Finally, the specificity of the metrical structure of this group of songs suggests that, if they were to be sung, they may have shared a melody, like many portmanteau melodies for sequences; the performance, accompanied by the *vielle*, of devotional and secular texts seems to have been similar.[19]

If melody is transmitted essentially through memory in such cycles, it can be said that parodic texts themselves depend on their readers' recollection of their models. In terms of the troubadour lyric, the importance of memory and recollection in composition, performance and transmission makes the variety of parodic rewriting especially interesting.[20] The intertextual competitiveness between Marcabru and Peire d'Alvernha is one form of rewriting, in which the speaker and audience's memory is invoked only in terms of the immediate models to hand. The two *sirventes* addressed to *joglars* by Guerau de Cabrera and Guiraut de Calanson, however, are based on a very different, and explicit, treatment of memory. They are in fact texts that are bound to a cultivation of memorization, in their use of the role of the *joglar* as conduit for transmission, and in their development of this *topos* into a didactic (or pseudo-didactic) text.

No one has yet provided a satisfactory interpretation of 'Cabra juglar', 'Fadet juglar' and their successor by Bertran de Paris, 'Gordo, ieu fai un bon sirventes l'an'. Pirot's study of their content did not reach a solid conclusion about their purpose. These poems share their basic scenario with a satirical subgenre known as the *sirventes joglaresc*: a monologue by a patron or troubadour who rebukes a *joglar* for his lack of skill, talent or appeal. However, whereas these pieces tend to be an invective of moderate length, designed to amuse the audience through their accumulation of insults, the three poems mentioned above are mostly made up of a long list of narratives, ranging in genre from Classical myth to Arthurian romance. This didactic aspect caused the texts to be labelled *ensenhamens au jongleur*, a definition rejected by Don Monson.[21] They are not destined to socialize or correct the behaviour of a social equal, and do not display an explicit ethical agenda. It would be tempting to read them as a carnivalized *ensenhamen*, in which the correction of morals and manners has been replaced by purely aesthetic criteria, with a strong edge of mockery aimed at a figure akin to a court fool.[22] This would not, however, explain why the poems are chiefly made up of a list of 'stories', linked by repetitive anaphora, structured as a chain of three-line versicles.

Most scholars have concluded that no single *joglar* could be expected to know the enormous repertoire presented in these lists, and have labelled the texts as a marginal, and somewhat tedious, example of a *gap*. The formal link between the poems to Cabra and Fadet and Marcabru's 'D'aisso lau Dieu' would support a reading of the invective as a form of boast. However, the *gap* genre does not, as a rule, degenerate into lists of texts. The interpretative difficulty of the three poems to *joglars* lies in their length and their apparent lack of purpose.

One possible interpretation of these texts may be reached by relating them not to the troubadour corpus of *sirventes*, but to Peire de Courbian's *Thezaur*. This text includes an analogous list which presents a repertoire of texts, but is structured as the speaker's direct boast about his own extensive repertoire. Peire lists material from the *romans antiques*, the *Roman d'Alexandre* and Arthurian material. Peire presents his extensive store of knowledge as 'mos tesaurs e mos amassamens', a personal treasure which replaces any need he might have for wealth. It is also of course directly related to the use of the term *thesaurus*, meaning 'storehouse' or 'treasure', which has been discussed by Mary Carruthers as a widespread image for for a well-stocked memory, a 'thesaurus sapientiae' or 'thesaurus eloquentiae'.[23]

Carruthers's study of medieval memorial culture and its related texts suggests that the *sirventes* to *joglars* could be read as mnemonic documents. Rather than being mere lists, such repetitive texts, in which narratives are alluded to through quick references, may have been 'heuristic devices'. The division of pieces of information into short units that may be easily learned, arranged in a flexible 'chain', and a repetitive formal basis, are typical elements of the memorization techniques laid out by writers prior to *c.*1240.[24] The list format is a device that makes it easy to skip between sections at will, and resembles the columns advocated by Hugh of Saint-Victor (*c.*1130). Where writers on *memoria* advised the creation of a 'background' based on a familiar social scene, and of recollection cues based on vivid or violent images, the texts present a dramatic scenario and invective. Each narrative is alluded to by the name of its protagonist (its *titulus*) and a key element. For example, Guerau de Cabrera tells Cabra 'Ni sabs d'Aiolz/ com anet solz' [nor do you know about Aiol, of how he went alone] (vv. 23–4), alluding to the scene at the opening of the romance of *Aiol*, in which the lone youth is mocked by townspeople. The purpose of such memorization is to facilitate composition or oratory, offering rapid references for the structuring of an argument.

An important feature of troubadours' references to knowledge of a song, the focus on the knowledge of the *incipit*, *titulus* or opening was derived from the memorization of the Psalms, a crucial qualification for a *clericus*.[25] It may be seen in a song to Mary, where Lanfranc Cigala asserts that his belief in the Virgin birth is supported by his detailed knowledge of at least one text, which he refers to by an incipit serving as a title:

> e.l ver salm que comensa:
> 'credo' crei tot
> de mot en mot.
> (*PC* 282, 2, vv. 93–5)

[In the true Psalm beginning 'Credo', I believe everything, word for word.]

Lanfranc is probably referring to the 'Psalter of Mary', which included the *Credo* and other prayers and had spread among the laity thanks to the mendicant orders by his time.[26]

For the speaker of these texts, the purpose of learning these *tituli* is to enable the *joglar* to perform texts with speed and success:

> Sapchas trobar
> e gen tombar
> e ben parlar e jocs partir.
> (vv. 13–15)

[Know how to compose and to tumble well, and to speak well and make *jeux partis*.]

In Guiraut de Calanson's poem, Fadet is informed of the skills required of him as an accomplished *joglar*: he must play an adequate number of musical instruments (vv. 13–42), wear a red beard as a mask and show puppets, dogs and monkeys (vv. 41–63), turn cartwheels, walk the tightrope (vv. 64–9), and tell numerous tales (vv. 73–226). Guiraut's *vida* states that he was an unsuccessful Gascon *joglar* who composed 'cansos maestradas desplazens e descorts d'aquella saison' [well-composed but displeasing *cansos* and *descorts* in the style of that time] (*BS*, XXV), which implies that the advice may not have been one-sided.

All the texts under scrutiny, with the exception of Peire de Courbian's *Thezaur* (*c.*1230–50), are datable to before or around the year 1200. This would make them precede the revival by Scholastic writers of Aristotle's and others' 'arts' of memory, which Carruthers locates at around 1240.[27] Prior to this change, traditional methods of memorization are presented by Hugh of Saint-Victor and Thierry of Chartres as a grid method in which single words or images function as cues in a visual field divided into thematic columns. There is support for the use of this method in Occitan-speaking lands in the prologue to a translation of the apocryphal Gospel of Nicodemus, which sets out a division of material into thematically labelled columns, 'catre colonas/ autas e fortz' [four columns, tall and strong], the first for prophets, the second for evangelists, the third for commentaries. The fourth column seems to be the text presented, a vernacular translation of a sacred text (Paris BN fr. 1745, f. 105). This model seems very similar to that set out by John of Garland in his *Parisiana poetria*, composed in the 1230s.[28]

The transfer of traditional mnemotechnique into written form in the thirteenth century has been attributed to the development of new preaching methods. The vogue for the thematic sermon, which relies on an extensive and flexible knowledge of citations, is connected to the cultivation of arts of memory by the Dominican order. However, another receptive community for such techniques was to be found in the notaries and lawyers of Italy and (by extension) southern France, for whom public speaking was becoming more important.[29] This relationship between preachers on the one hand, and literate practitioners of secular and vernacular speech on the other, may explain the cultivation of similar texts by troubadours from this social group, such as Peire Cardenal, for sermons and invective.

Further evidence that the two *sirventes* to *joglars* are related to mnemotechnique may be found in the suggestion by some troubadours that *joglars* themselves were regarded as storage devices. The anonymous song 'Gioglaretz, quant passaretz' (*PC* 461, 142) contains the following strange statement:

Ceu darre un moi descle
Sen carta qen teregle
Poi scriver una tal cobla
Sun daquist moti non si dubla.
(vv. 4–7)

These lines have been translated by Amelia Van Vleck as: 'I would give a barrel of rye [...] if, on a page which in you I rule, I could write such a stanza that not one of these rhymes is duplicated.'[30] This is tantamount to the troubadour promising to 'write' his song inside the *joglar*, whom he treats as a human songbook. The *joglar* is often addressed as the human repository of the song, which will be transmitted through him, for better or worse. In the case of the following song by Giraut de Bornelh, it is clear that such a 'container' could be difficult to manage:

Ditz tu que non remanras
S'eu t'o coman?
Vai doncs, e si.t prec del chan
Que no.l peiurs,
Coras que.t sufrajna
Bos albercs.
(*PC* 242, 79, Sharman, XXXI, vv. 51–6)

[Are you saying you won't stay if I tell you to? Go then, and I beg you of the song: don't spoil it when you don't find a decent lodging.]

This anxious relationship between the poem and the uncontrollable body in which it is stored can be seen as the source of the aggression towards *joglars* in some songs.[31] If the *joglar* is ignorant, he will spoil the effect of the words he bears; if his memory fails, he will lose them altogether. Guerau de Cabrera's *sirventes* opens with a salvo of references to his own performance:

> Cabra juglar
> non pusc mudar
> q'eu non chan, pos a mi sap bon;
> e volrai dir,
> senes mentir,
> e comptarai de ta faison.
> (vv. 1–6)

[Cabra, *joglar*, I cannot stop myself singing, for it pleases me to do so; and I would like to recite without lying, and to tell about your style.]

The list runs its course, linked by the repetition of negative statements, until Cabra (the Goat) is sent on his way with an insult assimilating the hapless *joglar* to his lecherous homonym: 'Va, Cabra, boc/ que be.t conoc/ Que te vi urtar al mouton' [Go, Cabra, he-goat, for I know you well: for I have seen you butting the sheep] (v. 214–16). This brutal ending implies performance, since it seems to require the presence of the offending minstrel.

Despite Guerau de Cabrera's insistence on oral performance, the *contrafactum* by Guiraut de Calanson indicates that the text was passed on in written form. He also suggests that it depended on memorization, and that reading was not the sole part of the process:

> E.m gart dels motz
> be de trastotz,
> de sels qu'En Giraut fes escrir,
> no sai lo cart,
> mas l'una part
> t'en dirai segon mon albir.
> (vv. 7–12)

[And I beware of the words, indeed of all those that En Guerau ordered to be written down; I don't know a quarter of them, but I will tell you one part of them according to my opinion.]

This troublesome passage differs in *R*, where lines 7–8 present a more visual angle again:

e gardals motz
be tras qe totz
de sels qen Gr. fes escrir.

[And look at the words, well [better?] drawn-out than all those En Guerau ordered to be written down.]

Here, the term 'tras' may be related to 'traire', a verb with a vast range in Occitan (to pull out, remove, tear, throw or hurl) which can also be read as 'to draw out'. This term in turn is used in its Latin form (*tractare*) to express the composition and the 'drawing out' of learned citations from *florilegia*, for the purposes of sermon composition.[32] Guiraut's boast is that his text, which the *joglar* can view, outdoes its predecessor in the repertoire it provides. His joking admission of a failure of memory (which would make him the equal of the reviled Cabra) appears to be compounded by the rest of the text, which is not a repetition of its model, but a parallel replica. It is also its opposite: where Cabra is told he does not know things, Fadet is ordered to learn them.

The lack of precision espoused by Guiraut illustrates the distinction made between *recitare*, the repetition word-for-word of learned material, and the preferred method of memorizing for the sense of a given passage, known as *retinere et dicere*.[33] Contrary to expectation, rote learning seems to have been considered the inferior skill, since it fails to allow flexibility and creativity in recollection. For both Guerau de Cabrera and Guiraut de Calanson, the *joglar*'s art consists of a skilful improvisation on the basis of a core of memorized material, which may be accessed through these repertoires. Their insistence on the importance of *saber* does not, however, imply that the *joglar* should have rote-learned his narratives. On the contrary, the ability to *retinere et dicere*, to retain and tell dynamically, is set above that of recitation.

Guiraut de Calanson seems to provide an example of how the repertoire may be used. At the close of 'Fadet juglar', the speaker breaks with the structure of anaphoric repetition after a reference to Amor:

Sapchas d'amor,
com vol' e cor
e com vai nuda ses vestir.
(vv. 202–4)

[Know about Love, how she flies and runs, and how she goes naked, unclothed.]

This is developed into a further twenty-one lines on the theme of Amor's three arrows, the four steps to reach her, and her deceitfulness (vv. 205–25). This section ends the list (*D* inserts an additional three-line versicle on the phoenix, v. 226–8) and the poem closes with a dedication to the young king of Aragon (vv. 229–43). If the text is a series of mnemotechnical *notulae*, Guiraut has ended it with a demonstration of how the single reference to the image of a naked Amor may cue a store of material about love and its ways.

This last section is proof that the text is a *thesaurus sapientiae*. A *canso* composed by Guiraut de Calanson, 'Celeis cui am de cor e de saber' (*PC* 243, 2),[34] uses the same elements in the same order to construct a different poem. The *canso* presents an allegorical depiction of a feminine 'menor tertz d'amor' (v. 4), who fires three arrows endowed with specific powers (vv. 11–16), is attained by four steps (v. 29), deceives her adherents and goes naked (vv. 46–7). All her kin are born of fire (vv. 47–8), which is similar to the phoenix that closes the development on Amor in 'Fadet joglar'. This allegorical *canso* is dedicated to Guillem de Montpellier (d. 1202) and sent to him without reference to a *joglar* as its bearer.

This did not exhaust the potential for 'drawing out' of the material cued by the short versicle on naked Amor. Guiraut Riquier later composed an extensive gloss on Guiraut's *canso*, on the orders of Enric, count of Rodez (Pfaff, LXXXIV). This 947-line text, dated January–February 1280 (vv. 20–45), was composed on the basis of a written version of the *canso* (vv. 53–4) which he says was initially performed in the court of Le Puy (v. 191). Guiraut Riquier glosses the *canso* in the manner of a preacher: he divides the song into its *coblas* after an exposition of the meaning of its title, the 'menor tertz d'amors'. Each *cobla* is presented in turn, and followed by his commentary of individual lines and phrases in terms of their degree of veracity. The reference to the allegorical figure's nakedness is decried as an uncourtly image implying both madness and poverty (vv. 789–804). The text is peppered with references to spiritual authority (the first 'terz' of Amor is, of course, spiritual) and ends with a Latin dedication to its scribe. Guiraut Riquier's *expositon* is followed by a short, highly ironic text which claims to be an endorsement by Enric of Rodez of the version signed by Guiraut Riquier. Dated July 1285 (vv. 31–4), it states that Guiraut de Calanson's *canso* was handed to four troubadours to be glossed, and that Riquier's is the version that has been approved by sealed letter, granting him *auctoritat* (v. 25).

There is more than a faint possibility that Guiraut Riquier's *expositio* may be a parody of a commentary on divine Scripture, and the irony of the *carta sagelada* [sealed letter] approving it seems to reinforce this. The invective *sirventes* composed by Guerau de Cabrera becomes the *thesaurus eloquentiae* for Guiraut de Calanson's own storehouse of memorized material, triggered by his imperfect memorization of it. In turn, this produces two more texts, a *canso* and a lengthy gloss. That this chain of interacting texts should end with a parodic *carta sagelada* seems to constitute a neat ending for the play between preaching and minstrelry that characterizes it.

Guiraut Riquier may have been familiar with 'Fadet joglar', which he alludes to in his *Suplicatio* of 1274 (Pfaff, LXXIX), asking the king of Castille to distinguish between the ranks of *joglars*. He notes that at the start of *ioglaria*, joglars were travelling entertainers who juggled balls, showed monkeys and puppets or played instruments (vv. 579–99); these were distinguished from troubadours who told tales of good deeds in song and praised good men (vv. 600–4). He regrets that nowadays there is a new class of entertainers who seek to do both (vv. 616–50). Guiraut's *Suplicatio* is responded to by the king's *Declaratio* (Pfaff, LXXV) in which the term *doctor de trobar* is offered for those troubadours who compose *vers* and *cansos*, as opposed to the *trobadors* who compose *coblas*, *dansas* and *sirventes* (vv. 296–317, 356–75). The chain of three songs presented above also presents the new hierarchy of *joglaria*: Fadet, a mere *joglar*, is informed how he may acquire the material that Guiraut de Calanson, the *trobador*, can use to compose his *cansos*. Meanwhile, the *doctor de trobar* Guiraut Riquier applies his skills to producing a gloss on the *canso*. In his *Suplicatio*, Guiraut presents *clergues* as the most diverse and ambitious name to be had (vv. 171–242); in his treatment of Guiraut de Calanson's *canso*, he has proved himself to be not simply a learned poet, but a qualified one too.

There remains a major question to be answered after this section. If this corpus usurps the form of liturgical or para-liturgical chant, twisting it into a series of parodies and counter-parodies which engage in a debate over knowledge, yet appear to have no centre, its purpose remains obscure. Given the variety of interpretations to which vernacular texts were open, a series of mocking songs such as those studied above could be read as blasphemous, parodic or moralizing. It remains to be seen what the effect would have been of a troubadour or a *joglar* masquerading as the secularized or defrocked clerk he so often was, especially in terms of the competitive rewritings in which these songs seem to engage.

Notes to Chapter 3

1. Alfred Jeanroy, *Les Origines de la poésie lyrique en France au Moyen Age* (Paris: Champion, 1925), 364–77; Pirot, *Recherches*, 97–8.
2. Pirot, *Recherches*, 546–62; Lejeune, 'La forme de *l'ensenhamen au jongleur*'.
3. Zufferey, *Recherches linguistiques*, 15–17.
4. Leo Treitler, 'Oral, Written and Literate Process in the Transmission of Medieval Music', *Speculum* 56 (1981), 471–91 (473).
5. Mary Carruthers, *The Book of Memory: A Study of Memory in Medieval Culture* (Cambridge: Cambridge University Press, 1990), 264, from Hugh of Saint-Victor, 'De Tribus Maximis Circumstantiis Gestorum' (*c.*1130), Appendix A.
6. Carruthers, *Book of Memory*, 93–5, 112–13, 185–8.
7. John of Salisbury, cited by Carruthers, *Book of Memory*, 113; Treitler, 'Oral, Written and Literate Process', 488–90.
8. Van der Werf, *Extant Troubadour Melodies*, 3, 6, 9, 11–14, 17–20, 29–30.
9. Masters, *Esthétique et manuscripture*, 205–11.
10. Vincent Pollina, *'Si Cum Marcabrus Declina': Studies in the Poetics of the Troubadour Marcabru* (Modena: STEM Mucchi, 1991), 29–31.
11. See Zufferey, *Recherches linguistiques*, for the compilation and dating of *IK*.
12. Legge, 'La versification', 639–43, cited by Pirot, *Recherches*, 102–3. See also Legge, *Anglo-Norman Literature and its Background*, 180–2.
13. Lavaud, *Peire Cardenal*, 530.
14. Hermann Suchier (ed.), *Zwei Altfranzösische Reimpredigten* (Halle: Niemeyer, 1949), 68, vv. 1–6.
15. F. J. Tanquerey (ed.), *Le Roman des Romans et le Sermon en Vers (Oyez, seignurs, sermun): Deux poèmes moraux anglo-français* (Paris: Champion, 1922).
16. Edmund Max Stengel (ed.), *Elie's de Wincestre, eines Anoynymus, und Everarts Übertragungen des Disticha Catonis* (Marburg: Elwert, 1886); Legge, *Anglo-Norman in the Cloisters*, 13–16.
17. See D'Arco Silvio Avalle, *La letteratura medievale in lingua d'Oc nella sua tradizione manoscritta. Problemi di critica testuale* (Turin: Einaudi, 1961).
18. See Cingolani, 'The *sirventes-ensenhamen*'; Pirot, *Recherches*.
19. Tito Saffioti, *I Giullari in Italia: Lo spettacolo, il pubblico, i testi* (Milan: Xenia, 1990), 119–21.
20. See the extensive study by Amelia Van Vleck, *Memory and Recreation in Troubadour Lyric*.
21. Monson, *Les 'Ensenhamens' occitans*, 156–66.
22. Maurice Lever, *Le Sceptre et la marotte: Histoire des fous de cour* (Paris: Fayard, 1983).
23. Carruthers, *Book of Memory*, 33–5. In Peire Vidal's *sirventes* 'Pos ubert ai mon ric tezaur' (*PC* 364, 38, Anglade, XLV), the troubadour presents a display of rhetorical virtuosity, cf. *PSW*, VIII, 219–20. See also Matthew Bardell, 'The allegorical landscape: Peire Vidal's 'ric thesaur''.
24. Carruthers, *Book of Memory*, 150–2, Appendix A.
25. Van Vleck, *Memory and Recreation*, 48–50; Carruthers, *Book of Memory*, 82–6.
26. Marina Warner, *Alone of all her Sex: The Myth and Cult of the Virgin Mary* (London: Picador, 1983), 360. Waldensians were condemned for substituting titles for the incipit of memorized psalms: Menache, *Vox Dei*, 239–40.

27. Carruthers, *Book of Memory*, 145–55 (150). See also Janet Coleman, *Ancient and Medieval Memories: Studies in the Reconstruction of the Past* (Cambridge: Cambridge University Press, 1992).
28. Bartsch, *Chrestomathie*, col. 409, vv. 14–30, from MS Paris fr. 1745, f. 105.
29. See also Pfeffer, *Proverbs in Medieval Occitan Literature*, 12–33.
30. Van Vleck, *Memory and Recreation*, 57–8.
31. William D. Paden, 'The Role of the *Joglar* in Troubadour Lyric Poetry', in *Chrétien de Troyes and the Troubadours: Essays in Memory of Leslie Topsfield*, ed. Peter S. Noble and Linda M. Paterson (Cambridge: St Catharine's College, 1984), 669–85; Van Vleck, *Memory and Recreation*, 71–3.
32. Carruthers, *Book of Memory*, 108, 176.
33. Carruthers, *Book of Memory*, 89–90.
34. Text and discussion in de Riquer, *Los Trovadores*, ii. 1081–4.

CHAPTER 4

Rewriting and the Role of Serious Parody

The author or performer of parody tends to occupy a subordinate place, not simply as a copyist of the model, but also as its envious spectator or pupil. The metaphors applied to the author of parody show a tendency to see the performance as parasitic or criminal; the terms 'vampire', 'cannibal', 'thief' or 'usurper' convey a negative vision of parody hard to reconcile with its depiction elsewhere as licensed play.[1] When two poets engage in combative rewriting, this aggression cannot be far from the surface, as the dialogue between Peire d'Alvernha and his predecessor Marcabru will show.

Paul Lehmann's study of Latin parody offers the possibility of reading *either* ludic *or* polemical intentionality into texts. For example, the lament of Job, 'Versa est in luctum cithara mea et organum in vocem flentium' [My harp has been tuned for a dirge, my flute to the voice of those who weep] (Job 30:31) can become an erotic complaint, 'Vertitur in luctum/ organum amoris', or an introduction to a satirist's song: 'Versa est in luctum/ cythara Waltheri'.[2]

Both parodies are secularizations of sacred text, but it is not clear if they would have been received as a profanation of the text concerned. While the author of the erotic song is punning on school-learned images of grieving, Walter of Châtillon invites the spectator or reader to align his suffering as a satirist with the sufferings of Job. In so doing, he illustrates the parodist's characteristic usurpation of an authoritative voice by making use of a commonly known text, and places himself as the object of the parody. Similarly, another song by Walter opening 'Ecce sonat en aperto/ Vox clamantis in deserto' (see Isaiah 40:3) equates his reprobate persona as a goliard with that of a prophet preaching unheeded in the desert. This image is also adopted by Marcabru in the tornada of a violent invective poem, using the image of the self-scourging hermit to illustrate his alienation from society (*PC* 398, 32, XXXI, vv. 91–3).[3]

In the absence of sufficient evidence from the Middle Ages, the degree of shock value ascribed to such performances may be analysed via modern examples of parody of the sacred. Comic parody sometimes consists of the placing of sacred objects in inappropriate places, or the speaking of religious words out of context. The comic effect in such cases appears to counterbalance any potential for blasphemy. Similarly, the commonplace parodies of Christmas carols by twentieth-century British schoolchildren are not usually received as profanations of sacred texts, but as play on familiar melodies and words encountered in numerous non-religious contexts.

One interesting study of the parodic treatment of the sacred has been Maria Luisa Meneghetti's reading of the 'Estornels' poems by Marcabru in relation to a bilingual sequence narrating the Annunciation.[4] The starling in Marcabru's songs is read here as a parodied archangel Gabriel, announcing himself as 'auzels' rather than *angelus*. The songs are replete with travestied Scriptural citations: 'Denan totas va triada' [She goes chosen before all other women], is explained as a burlesqued version of the antiphonal phrase 'benedicta tu in mulieribus' (Luke 1:28).[5]

For Meneghetti, such a travesty of the Annunciation, in which the dialogue between God, archangel and Virgin is transformed into a negotiation over sex between a lover, a bird and a woman of notorious virtue, should not be read as blasphemy. It is rather a playful treatment of a Marian hymn written in two languages, an *avant-garde* composition which may have been performed for the Poitiers court at which Marcabru was active until *c.*1137.

The Annunciation was sometimes enacted in liturgical dramas which involved stylized gestures, characterization and costume. In a thirteenth-century version from Padua, the antiphon 'Benedicta tu in mulieribus' was performed by a clerk representing Elizabeth, as he knelt before the clerk playing Mary, his hands placed on the other actor's body. Such dramatic performances could provide both entertainment and copious material for parody; indeed, Peter Dronke has noted that the abrupt changes of voice in the Saint-Martial piece imply performance by several people of a dialogue between Virgin and angel which has a strong erotic edge.[6]

Laura Kendrick's study of Marcabru's poetry as the collected corpus of a thinly disguised enterprise of ecclesiastical propaganda, while attractive, seems overly reductive when applied to such songs as these.[7] Literacy in twelfth-century Occitania, as in other parts of Europe, came through the learning of Psalms, Biblical citations and the *Disticha Catonis*, which would make matters of morality, doctrine and divine authority familiar rather than inherently politicized.[8] Explicit references to liturgy and doctrine are interesting in that they question and attempt to resolve issues of authoritative speech when framed or voiced by a preacher's persona, or in a metre familiar from devotional practice; in turn, parodied versions of familiar or fashionable texts are open to a variety of interpretations.

The identification of parodies as opposed to *contrafacta* is also a thorny issue when dealing with troubadour songs. One 21-line stanzaic structure (Frank 101) is used with the same rhymes and metrical structure by a Franciscan singing to the Virgin (Fraire Menor, *PC* 159, 1), and by Gui d'Ussel for a *cobla* (*PC* 194, 16).

As was noted in the introduction, Gui d'Ussel was a canon of secular tastes who was eventually banned from practising *trobar*. This implies that he was irreverent enough to adapt a devotional song in a secular form, but records show that Gui became an adult around the year 1195 and was dead by 1225 (*BS*, XXII). If, as his *vida* states, he gave up the composition and performance of songs altogether on the orders of the Papal legate, a likely date would be the enforcement of the decree of the Council of Montpellier of 1214, which forbade clerks to indulge in 'dominare' (*domneis*) with ladies. If he did retire from composition around the year 1214, this would make his Franciscan model a very early example of a Marian hymn in the vernacular.

One possibility is that the Fraire Menor copied Gui's *cobla* and rewrote it as a devotional song. Serious or sacred parody is a common device from the Counter-Reformation onwards, which has been extended by some critics to include twentieth-century texts. One form of serious parody found from the Middle Ages onwards is rewriting *a lo divino*, which was often practised by mystical poets.[9] This consists of the rewriting of a popular ballad by keeping its form but inserting devotional content. The process is not simply *contrafactum* work, because awareness of the hypotext is never lost or obscured.

Peire d'Alvernha, who was active between *c.*1150 and *c.*1170, predates the mendicant orders by a good half-century, yet is the author of five devotional songs, which are composed in a form typical of troubadour lyric poetry.[10] There is also a disputed attribution to 'Dieus verais, a vos mi ren' (Zenker, *PC* 27, 46), a poem with Marian content which seems to be of later date. Peire's poems are varied: 'De dieu non posc pauc ben parlar' (*PC* 323, 14, Zenker, XVII), a moralizing poem of praise, contrasts with 'Deus vera vida verais' (*PC* 323, 16, XVIII) and 'Lauzatz sia Emanuel' (*PC* 323, 21, XIX), two poems displaying a more sophisticated technique. 'Deus vera vida' uses the preaching device of setting scenes from the Old Testament in dialogue with scenes from the New. 'Lauzatz sia Emanuel' is an exploration of Trinitarian doctrine, expressed as a prayer. The song 'Gent es, mentr'om n'a lezer' (*PC* 323, 18, XV) announces the speaker's withdrawal from the world, while 'Cui bon vers agrad' a auzir' (*PC* 323, 13, XVI) is a meditation on death which ends with an exhortation to prayer (vv. 50–4). This last song is explicitly intended to function as a sermon, and features advice for listeners:

> Ben deuria pessar morir
> qui dregz uelhs garda sus. lo vout
> cossi dieus per nos a guerir
> receup mort, e pus mort aucis
> selhui que per nos venc en crotz;
> tug morrem, qu'avers no.ns gueris
> negun al temps plus que fes Jop.
> (vv. 36–42)

[He should indeed think of dying who keeps his eyes set on the image of how God, in order to cure us, received death, and then the one who was on the cross for us killed death; we shall all die, for wealth does not cure anyone of it at the time, any more than it cured Job.]

Peire's references to the 'curative' powers of Christ is a detail which seems similar to the idea of Christ as 'celestis medicus', a theme Geneviève Hasenohr has traced in the sermons of Geoffrey Babio, bishop of Bordeaux (1136–58). According to Hasenohr, the vernacular sermon collections compiled in the abbey of Saint-Martial-de-Limoges are at least in part derived from his sermons, compiled for diffusion by the Benedictine monks for use in pastoral work.[11] The abbey was probably a key player in the diffusion of preaching techniques across Occitania in the twelfth century, since it controlled sixty-five churches, and its priories administered up to forty-five parishes to which it appointed priests. Hasenohr suggests it also provided training in catechetical preaching in the vernacular.[12] Peire's devotional songs seem to show the influence of such texts.

Peire closes his *memento mori* in 'Cui bon vers agrad' a auzir' with a comment that seems to point to written diffusion, and performance using a text as a prop, if not a source: 'Tot jorn vos poiria legir;/ mas preguem cel qu'es caps e fis/ que.ns garde del enfernal potz' [I could read to you all day, but let us pray to Him who is the beginning and the end, that He might keep us from the infernal pit] (vv. 50–2). This interesting detail seems to point to performance in which the speaker is reading from a written document, emulating a preacher speaking with reference to an open book.

It is not possible to reach firm conclusions about the social status of Peire d'Alvernha. Despite Bernart Marti's comment about his past as a canon (cited in the Introduction, above), his *vida* describes a man of bourgeois origin who enjoyed a completely secular and peripatetic career until 'el fetz penitensa e mori' [he repented and died], which may refer to a late conversion (*BS*, XXXIX). The version in *R* says he entered an unspecified religious order. The devotional texts have not been dated. Given the popularity of the Cistercian order with troubadours of the late twelfth century, it would seem plausible that Peire, like Bertran de Born and Bernart de Ventadorn, might have retired into a house of this order. It is certainly tempting to suggest that the devotional poems might be the product of a poet living on the cusp of the secular and sacred worlds.[13]

Peire d'Alvernha also seems to have practised serious parody, if it is assumed that his two-part narrative of a lover's dialogue with a messenger-nightingale is a rewritten version of Marcabru's 'Estornels' cycle (*PC* 323, 23a and 23b).[14] Set in the context of his devotional *vers*, Peire's 'Be m'es plazen' may be read as a serious parody of Marcabru's 'D'aisso lau Dieu', attempting to rewrite the scabrous *gap* as a devotional text, perhaps under the influence of Cistercian thought.

The appropriation of *joglar* material and techniques appears to have been fully developed in the generations after Peire d'Alvernha by the Franciscan friars. In the *Vita Seconda* of St Francis of Assisi, Tommaso da Celano describes Francis miming the bowing of a *vielle* and singing the praises of God, in French.[15] The term 'joculatores Domini' used by Cesarius of Heisterbach applies to the friars' adoption of minstrels' songs, emotivity, mime and music in preaching, perhaps in competition with minstrels for popular audiences, as Saffioti has suggested. In turn, popes kept jesters who recited parodic sermons and who were, in some cases, friars.[16] While this explains the action of the Fraire Menor, it is also interesting to examine a dialogue which appears to predate this fashion by half a century.

Marcabru's 'D'aisso lau Dieu' is a song to which Peire d'Alverna's 'Be m'es plazen' is inextricably tied. Linda Paterson reads the two songs as a debate on poetics, noting that Peire's alternative to Marcabru's *amors* is 'intentionally inexplicit'. She suggests that Peire substitutes his 'purely poetic method', which privileges 'openness and vagueness of expressions', for Marcabru's discussion of his own antagonistic poetics and concern for individuated concepts.[17] The imprecision of the alternatives espoused by Peire leads Paterson to base her interpretation on the additional stanzas in *chansonnier a*, which enables her to approach the text as a secular discussion of *amor de lonh*, mentioned in the *a* version *tornada*. Leslie Topsfield, meanwhile, uses the *a* stanzas too, and reads the song as an attempt by Peire to break with the enslavement to undisciplined, physical desires, and to seek a 'secure contentedness of the individual within himself and within society'. Rejecting the previous interpretations of this poem as the announcement of withdrawal into spiritual contemplation or isolation, Topsfield prefers to underline the extent to which 'Be m'es plazen' is an 'amalgam' of the poetics of Marcabru, Guilhem IX and Jaufre Rudel. He states that the ambiguity of the song lies in the fact that the poem is constructed on 'three planes of love, physical, imaginary and spiritual'.[18]

Simon Gaunt has noted that whereas Marcabru attacks a number of other poets, the bulk of Peire's parodic activity appears to be aimed competitively at Bernart de Ventadorn, reducing Bernart's persona to a set of shallow commonplaces.[19] By way of contrast, Marcabru is cited by Peire d'Alvernha as his admired 'master', the predecessor whom he uses to authorize his own poetry, and appears to be recuperated rather than mocked.[20] It is precisely this apparent wish on his part to clean up Marcabru's most savagely ironizing songs, the 'Estornels' songs and 'D'aisso lau Dieu', that demands attention in a discussion of parody.

Marcabru's *gap* constructs a voice which boasts of sexual mores similar to those of Guilhem IX's 'Companho' poems; as has been noted elsewhere, it seems to be a close parody of 'Companho, tant ai agut d'avols conres' (*PC* 185, 5, Pasero, III):[21]

> E dirai vos m'entendensa de que es:
> no m'azauta cons gardatz, ni gorcs ses peis,
> ni gabars de malvatz homes c'om de lor faitz non agues.[22]
>
> (vv. 4–6)

[And I'll tell you my understanding of the situation: I do not like a guarded cunt, nor a pond without fish, nor the bragging of evil men whose deeds do not match their words.]

Marcabru seems to have appropriated this 'gabars de malvatz homes' by creating a voice which embodies the complaints of Guilhem's speaker. Guilhem IX's song calls itself a *casteis* (v. 13), a chastisement or reproof, and uses didactic terminology in a parody of the proverbs and advice given by the wise man (the *savis hom*) of Latin wisdom literature:

> Pero dirai vos de con, cals es sa leis,
> com sel hom que mal n'a fait e peitz n'a pres;
> si c'autra res en merma, qui.n pana, e cons en creis.
> (vv. 10–12)

[But I'll tell you what the law of the cunt is, as a man who has done ill in this respect, and suffered worse; while another thing diminishes once you steal from it, the cunt grows.]

It may be worth pointing out here that the *Disticha Catonis* and other proverb collections used for school teaching were filled with advice on the control and management of women, especially wives. For example, a later Occitan translation of such proverbs, known as *Lo Savi*, contains the precept:

> E gara be la tua causa,
> que.l savi te la sua clausa.
> (col. 370)

[And keep your 'thing' well guarded, for the wise man keeps his own enclosed.]

Here, the advice about the containment of women's sexuality, usually presented as uncontrollable unless bridled by a man, is rewritten with irony, to emphasize the gratification which may come from the exploitation of another man's property. The speaker states that he feels aggrieved by the existence of men who place women under guard, not because this is a source of distress to the woman, but because this curtails his enjoyment of her unbridled sexual appetite:

> Senhers Dieus, quez es del mon capdels e reis,
> qui anc premiers gardet con, com non esteis?
> C'anc no fo mestiers ni garda c'a sidons estes sordeis.
> (vv. 7–9)

[Lord God, you who are lord and king of the world, why did he who first kept a cunt under guard not die? For there never was a service nor a custody that was worse to his lady.]

Misogynistic reduction of a woman to unbridled *con* is turned on its head; rather than a warning against feminine sexuality, the speaker uses it as an excuse for the unleashing of his own desires. If lords will insist on making their wives so tempting, it is only natural to enjoy the results:

> E sel qui no.n volra.n creire mos casteis
> an ho vezer pres lo bosc en un deveis:
> per un albre c'om hi tailla n'i naisson [ho] dos ho treis.
> (vv. 13–15)
>
> E quan lo bocx es taillatz, nais plus espes,
> e.l senher no.n pert son comte ni sos ses;
> a revers planh hom la tala, si.l dampn [...]
> (vv. 16–18)

[And as for him who does not heed my warnings, let him go and look in an enclosure, near the forest: for every tree that is cut down, two or three spring up.

And when the wood is pruned, it grows back thicker, and its lord won't lose his investment, nor his fees; lamenting destruction is wrong-headed, if [no?] damage [has been done].]

The *vers* is written in direct contradiction to certain familiar passages of moralizing literature. In the Book of Proverbs, the young male protagonist is depicted as the victim of an errant woman who, whether a prostitute or a wife, is presented as wandering the streets or sitting outside the door of her house, for example in Proverbs 9: 13–17, where she is placed in opposition to Sapientia as Stultitia, 'Mulier stulta et clamosa'. A stupid and noisy creature, it is she who calls men over to her, saying, 'Aquae furtivae dulciores sunt/ Et panis absconditus suavior' [Stolen waters are sweet, and bread got by stealth tastes even better].

The speaker of Marcabru's *gap* presents himself as a trickster figure, a seducer who keeps his wife locked away in order to enjoy the wives of others. The idea of adultery as 'aquae furtivae' and 'panis absconditus' appears in the song as a boast: what Stultitia offers the fool in the Book of Proverbs is precisely that which the speaker of this song is all too willing to enjoy:

De gignos sens
sui si manens
que mout sui greus ad escarnir;
lo pan del fol
caudet e mol
manduc, e lais lo mieu frezir.
(vv. 13–18)

[I am so rich in cunning senses that I am very harsh in my mockery; I eat the fool's bread, warm and soft, and leave mine to grow cold.]

Where Guilhem's *casteis* condemns the creation of 'guarded enclosures' where wives will increase in sexual appetite, Marcabru's fool rushes into the enclosures of others to enjoy the hunt, while making sure his own property is guarded. 'En l'autrui broill/ chatz cora.m voill' [In another's wood, I hunt as I please] (vv. 37–8), but:

Mos alos es
en tal deves
res mas ieu non s'en pot jauzir;
(vv. 43–5)

[My allod is in such a private hunting ground that no one save me can enjoy it.]

The *gap* ends with a threat. The speaker seems to warn his listeners that he may impregnate their own wives with alacrity, likening them to hapless birds condemned to endure the intrusion of this cuckoo:

Cascun si gart
c'ab aital art
mi fatz a viure e morir;
qu'ieu sui l'auzels
c'als estornels
fatz los mieus auzellos noirir.
(vv. 55–60)

[Let every man beware, for with such an art I intend to live and die; for I am the bird who makes the starlings raise my young.]

The speaker plays on the relationship between him and the man he is tricking. By entering his service, he can steal both his 'bread' and his possessions; he can also give him an unwanted heir. He will return to his own possessions (his wife) only once he finds himself denied the pleasure of theft (vv. 19–24). This sets the *gap* in opposition to the speaker of the 'Companho' songs, who asserts his right to his vassals' property and women. Marcabru's speaker only has one allod, which he chooses to guard jealously. He is, in fact, the man reviled by Guilhem IX for guarding his wife, and refuses to envisage the fluidity of exchange envisaged by the model text as the possible mitigation of guarding *con*. His, in any case, will not be allowed onto the open market.

Marcabru's *gap* presents a boast by a declaredly *malvatz hom*, whose sheer hyperbole may imply that his deeds do, indeed, not match his words. Guilhem IX's reference to the pool without fish (v. 5) is used elsewhere in a proverbial form by Marcabru to complain of empty promises from a patron to a troubadour (*PC* 293, 23, Dejeanne XXIII, vv. 22–3). In 'D'aisso lau Dieu', Guilhem's song is parodied by Marcabru in a literalization of the empty promises and bragging of a fraudster.

The sexual imagery of both songs is violent, but while Guilhem's envisages sexuality in terms of forcible containment through pruning and enclosure, Marcabru's song privileges a predatory and agonistic vision. The *gap* is full of images of man-to-man combat and humiliation, expressed in terms of phallic objects, such as sticks, clubs, hunting dogs and fencing weapons. The uncontrollable trees which Guilhem identifies as female sexuality running away from its owner despite his attempts at containment (vv. 15–18) are modified into phallic references to palisades and energetic husbandry. From a many-headed Hydra, the *con* becomes a passive object to be invaded, eaten or neglected, hunted or enclosed. Marcabru's description of an enclosed garden guarded against trespassers by what amounts to a speaking phallus is reminiscent of the Classical Latin *Priapeia*, as is the threatening tone maintained throughout the song.[23] Guilhem's song of the fearsome cunt receives a riposte from the combative phallus, asserting its superiority when it comes to wreaking havoc.

This usurper, occupying a subordinate or inferior social position to the model text, is close to the depiction of the parodic author by Bakhtin: 'The second voice, once having made its home in the other's discourse, clashes hostilely with its primordial host and forces him to serve directly opposing aims. Discourse becomes an arena of battle between two voices.'[24] Marcabru's song is a complex parody in that it challenges Guilhem's to a duel, fights it with countless references to combat, and asserts its victory by threatening to impose an unwanted child on the recipient, now a passive nest. It also appears to be spoken by a combination of the fool seduced by Stultitia from Scripture, and Guilhem's 'maistre certa' of the 'joc doussa' from *PC* 183, 2, Pasero VI (vv. 29–31).

Peire d'Alvernha's song, on the other hand, appears to defeat both its predecessors by rejecting sexuality altogether. In 'Be m'es plazen', love is depicted not in terms of obsessive sexual antagonism, but as a set of past and present relationships, which have burdened the speaker with concerns that distract him from his true focus: himself. The song has a disputed manuscript tradition.[25] Until 1900, it was known as an *unicum* in *C*, and edited as such by Rudolf Zenker. However *chansonnier a¹* contains a separate, longer version which appears to speak in terms of *amor de lonh*. Before the discovery of *chansonnier a¹*, Peire's song was read as a *contemptus mundi*, and the prelude to withdrawal into monastic seclusion. The new manuscript tradition unveiled by *a¹* changed the understanding of the poem radically.

The versions of the text in fragments *z* and *m*, edited in 1915 and 1939 respectively, repeat elements of the *a¹* version. It was tempting to dismiss the *C* version as a corrupt variant on the fuller text of *a¹ mz*, but this seemed to create more problems than it solved.[26] This situation led Antoine Tavera to abandon the idea that the *C* text was a later corruption, and to suggest that the song was reworked by Peire d'Alvernha in his own lifetime to suit two occasions.

Aniello Fratti's recent work on these problems of transmission led him to agree with Tavera's hypothesis, and to posit a hypertext transmitted from the start in two parallel versions. He produced a reconstructed version of 'Be m'es plazen' on this basis.[27] Fratti's parallel versions are not based on any one manuscript text; his version A of 'Be m'es plazen' is a pastiche or parody of Marcabru's *gap* with additional barbs aimed against Jaufre Rudel and Guilhem IX. Its speaker is an ironic persona, a failed version of Marcabru's bragging seducer. The second version, B, was produced on the occasion of Peire's withdrawal into monasticism, and the speaker is intended to be taken seriously in his expression of *contemptus mundi*.[28]

While Fratti's theory is seductive, it has several drawbacks. Versions A and B are both composites of the versions in all four manuscripts and require complex interpretative activity on the part of the reader, who must work through the manuscript tradition to identify the earlier, lost, forms of the poem. The intended recipient of this song is set the task of distinguishing between an ironic voice in A and a serious voice in B, when reading a text that is, in any case, a parody of an earlier piece. Also, Fratti does not explain why Peire d'Alvernha should have chosen this sarcastic attack on his predecessors as the best vehicle for the announcement of his conversion to a life of spiritual withdrawal. If this was his intention, it clearly failed to impress later performers, who preferred to conflate the two versions into a whole that fails to be convincingly repentant.

Fratti postulates two stages of parodic rewriting for 'Be m'es plazen'. The first may be read as a ludic parody of Marcabru, and the second is a serious parody of his own parodic text. In B, the speaker of A, whom Fratti reads as an opportunistic lover who has given up on women after a sequence of failed relationships, is rewritten *a lo divino* as a genuine penitent opting for the spiritual life. In response to Fratti's theory, I have chosen not to analyse either of his own suggested versions, but to read one extant manuscript version of the song, as an instance of a performance of the text. Consequently, I have chosen to edit the text below from *chansonnier C* only, ff. 179–80^r, in isolation from the texts of *a*^{1} *mz*, referring to Zenker's edition:

  Be m'es plazen
  e cossezen
qui s'ayzina de chantar,
  ab motz alquus
  serratz e clus
q'*o*m tem ja de vergonhar.

  Tan chai em bas
  q*ui* per compas
no sap lo segle demenar.
  Aquel hi falh
  que tan trassalh
que non puesca atras tornar.

  Ben es auras
  totz crestias
q'*e*l mezeis si vol encombrar,
  ni sobre.l cays,
  leva tal fays,
que corren no.l puesca portar.

  Qu'ieu cug e sen
  mon escien,
ieu vuelh vos o totz castiar:
  per trop captens
  val hom mot mens,
e.n ten hom plus vilh son afar.

Mai am un ort
serrat e fort
on hom non puesca ren emblar,
q*e* cent paras
sus en puegz plas
qu'autre las tenha ez ieu las guar.

Qu'arreire temps
ai amat ne*m*ps
e vuelh m'en atrazach layssar.
Non aura grat
qui m'a amat,
ni en cor m'avia d'amar.

Qu'ieu ai un cor
e un demor
e un ardit e un pessar,
e un amic
e un abric
e a cuy me vuelh autreyar.

Si mal m'en pren
per eys mon sen
cug a ma vida follejar.
Apres ma mort
no fass'om tort
d'aquo qu'ieu ai ad oblidar.

[It pleases me a great deal and concerns me that one should try to sing with specific, locked and closed words that one should fear shaming.

He falls down so much who doesn't know how to direct the secular world with moderation. Such a man fails who transgresses so much he doesn't know how to turn back.

Any Christian is mad who wishes to encumber himself; he lifts such a burden above his face that he'll not be able to carry it when running.

For I think and feel, assuredly, that I wish to reprove you all: for being too defensive, a man is worth far less and considers his torment to be viler.

I love a garden which is locked and fortified, from which nobody can steal anything, more than a hundred terrains up on flat hilltops, for another owns them and I guard them.

For in time past I have loved too much, and I wish to abandon this at once; whoever has loved me, or had it in their heart to love me, will not be thanked.

For I have one heart and one lodging, one passion and one suffering, and one friend and one shelter, to whom I wish to surrender myself.

If evil should come to me from this, despite my good sense, I think I'll have been foolish all my life. After my death, let no man blame me for that which I had to forget.]

Peire's song is explicitly concerned with penitence; it follows a statement that the song should be enclosed and secure with a warning that it should not be shamed, presumably by vulgarity. The second and third stanzas address a key image of penitential preaching, that of the sinner burdened by his sins and worldly concerns to the extent of losing his direction, and eventually of losing the path to salvation. The speaker announces his intention of reproving his audience, a mode of address similar to that of a preacher opening a denunciation of sin, as well as an echo of Guilhem's reference to his song as a *casteis* (see above, v. 13). The opening of this serious parody seems to state that this song may emulate the form of a bawdy song, but that it will be high-minded and an attempt to correct its listeners, and perhaps those of its hypotexts.

Peire's song functions by systematically controlling and denying the rhetorical freedom of its models. Whereas Marcabru's song displays a kaleidoscope of *colors* and *sens*, Peire's riposte to it reiterates the notion of a single unadorned unit, something which the version in *chansonnier C* emphasizes with the visually striking symbol it uses to render the word 'e' (vv. 37–42). Peire privileges a cautious selection of words in preference to multiple open terrains which may not fully be mastered. His declaration of faith amounts to an egocentric *credo* of self-protection.

Peire's rewriting of Marcabru's *gap* is tantalizingly similar to the technique for self-purgation outlined by Bernard of Clairvaux in his sermon on conversion, *De conversione ad clericos*, one version of which was delivered *c.*1139–40.[29] According to Janet Coleman's interpretation of this text, the would-be convert is encouraged to whitewash rather than erase his memories of his sinful past. Rather than rub out the 'ink' of sensual experience that stains the 'parchment', the penitent should strive to rewrite the text by censuring all past memories, after the successful shutting off of all his senses. Peire seems to echo such ideas in his devotional song 'Gent es, mentr'om n'a lezer' (*PC* 323, 18, XV):

> Pois dieus so.m laissa vezer
> en que puesc esser miraire
> de mo mielhs e.l sordeis raire.
> (vv. 22–4)

[For may God let me see in what I can be the beholder of the best in me, and erase the worst.]

This sermon is in tune with Bernard de Clairvaux's reformulation of knightly culture and aspirations into a sacred context, which he uses as a key device of his preaching. His sermons on the Song of Songs have been read as a reversal *a lo divino* of courtly love topoi, aiming at a corrective moral redefinition of Amors.[30] It also fits in with the apparent message of the last stanzas of Peire's song, when the speaker announces a withdrawal characterized by the shutting off of his senses and a renunciation of his past, whether lovers, friends or audience. This renunciation comes in the form of a conscious 'whitewashing' of Marcabru's song: Peire takes a text that seems to celebrate sensuality and excess, and whittles every image down to a single *amic* and a single garden.[31] The garden itself is accessible not through the combative aggression of the *gap*'s speaker, but through solitary spiritual effort; as Bernard of Clairvaux advises, 'you enter this garden not on foot but by deeply felt affections'.[32]

However, Peire does not follow this Cistercian model of conversion to the end; Bernard of Clairvaux advised the convert not to focus solely on himself, but to seek the well-being of his neighbours (*De conversione*, XIV, 29). Peire rejects his audience altogether, and states that he cares for neither overt nor concealed affection from others. He appears to present the speaker as a man with no need for any affirmation of identity through interaction with others, either through cautious alignment, or through outright antagonism; instead, he asserts that he has one single Other, and prefers to devote himself to his contemplation of and companionship with him, in one abode (vv. 40–2). This is more in keeping with what Caroline Walker Bynum has identified as the Cistercian and, indeed, monastic ideal of solitary contemplation of God with avoidance of implication in the lives of others.[33]

Guilhem IX's song simultaneously embraces and distances his audience, addressing them as fellow-men and companions, but warning that he wishes to keep certain aspects of his troubles a secret (vv. 1–3); this emphasizes the idea that the private sphere exists for the speaker, who is able to assert his superior rank in order to prevent himself being fully known. Marcabru's treats his audience as enemies and rivals, men he must threaten, challenge and destabilize with threats of cuckoldry, humiliation and defeat in verbal display. The fact that Peire's chosen companion is a masculine *amic* underlines the narcissism of his withdrawal, and its hope of fusion with a perfect companion, both equal and superior (v. 42). The audience itself is feared, in that he anticipates the disapproval this rejection of others may bring, and the possibility that such overt misanthropy may bring him trouble (vv. 43–8).

Peire's song in the *C* version ends with a veiled warning to the audience he has rejected: in maintaining their continued interest in him, they may be worsening his, and their own, folly (vv. 43–8). Both Marcabru's and Peire's songs conclude on a defiant note, threatening to implicate the audience in their respective follies, but while the *gap* threatens a life-or-death struggle (vv. 52–4), Peire considers others' interpretations of him only after his death (vv. 46–7). In distinct ways, both poems attempt to control their audience's perception of the speaker in action, and after he falls silent. Both are concerned with the construction of a speaking voice in response to Guilhem IX's model, which rests upon a debased moralizing voice, unable to deal with a *lex naturae* embodied by an all-encroaching female principle. Marcabru's response is to set up an antagonistic Priapus, devoted to dominating all others, male and female, while Peire presents the mirror image of this figure, a self-absorbed ascetic, concerned with an integrity achieved through the rejection of all emotional ties.

Peire's feminine terrains are as feared as those of his predecessors; he may watch over them, but he cannot control them (vv. 37–42). His rejection of the *con* addresses both its unbridled and its imprisoned aspects; he simply withdraws from such excessive activity, 'ai amat nemps' [I have loved too much] (v. 32). This again echoes Guilhem IX's song in its opening claim to disenchantment through long experience (vv. 1–2), but takes a different route, avoiding Guilhem's move into invective, and channelling his disgust into withdrawal. However, this ascetic is also a clerk imbued with Cistercian ideas of conversion which involve the rewriting of his past. He cannot erase his secular poetry, but he can purge it.

Intriguingly, Bernard of Clairvaux himself was accused of pride in his rhetoric, in an attack that is reminiscent of Bernart Marti's accusations against Peire d'Alvernha (*PC* 63, 6, Beggiato V, vv. 31–6). Having composed secular music and engaged in 'rhymed verse competitions' which enabled him to outshine his peers in his youth, Bernard, it was said, had become a preacher who used his talents to compose similarly frivolous texts, claiming them to be for God.[34] The declaredly penitential work may be a work of pride, too.

Peire's song attempts to close the intertextual chain, by shutting off the possibility of further dialogue: the speaker denies further communication and presents his own epitaph, having effectively shut his eyes to the possibility of future growth. This contrasts neatly with Marcabru's threat to produce bastard heirs and further combative dialogue; in keeping with Marcabru's sexual poetics, a lower-ranking speaker's usurpation of the Duke's possessions (his song) produces a barren child, and the end of the line.

Peire's 'purging' of 'D'aisso lau Dieu' raises the question how to read the poem. If attributed to Guilhem IX, the song would be interpreted literally as a boast; indeed, it almost seems that Peire has read the *gap* at face value and attempted to defeat it by quitting the proffered phallic competition altogether. The question of Peire's ironization of his poetic voice is a difficult one; his self-portrait in his poets' gallery indicates that he played on the persona of an arrogant poet (*PC* 323, 11, Zenker, XII), but the extent of his self-deprecation is questionable.[35] It may be argued that his serious parody of Marcabru reflects respect for his predecessor, but enacts a key performance of parody, defusing the power of the hypotext by rewriting it in order to negate its terms and impose closure upon it.

Peire d'Alvernha may be influenced by another Cistercian device, the use of inversion to express the monastic ideal. According to Caroline Walker Bynum, Bernard of Clairvaux took up the New Testament's interest in the reversal of language and values (1 Cor. 1:20), and used this idea to illustrate the choice of humility in the eyes of the materialistic laity, stating that monks are 'like acrobats and jugglers, who with heads down and feet up, stand or walk on their hands'.[36] By reversing secular values and texts, spiritual truth may be accessed. However, the process of divorcing form from content falters in Peire's song, in that his transition to a purely devotional sphere of reference does not quite work. If, as Fratti suggests, his intention was to write a corrected version of his own song, it was not successful in ensuring that the older, sinful, text was forgotten. This failure, if such it is, opens the way to Peire Cardenal's complete return to devotional concerns in the versified sermon 'Predicator', and to Guiraut de Calanson's adherence to a text that is literally and specifically about a fool's performance, audience and minstrelry. The texts that follow from Peire's attempt at recuperation are either declaredly devotional, or declaredly secular.

To close this chapter, it is worth citing Guillem de Berguedà's transgressive parody, the scurrilous 'Un trichaire' (*PC* 210, 22, Riquer, XVIII). A parodic attack on a priest named Rogier, who is said to be from Poitou, this is an unusual choice of subject for Guillem, most of whose invectives have been identified as attacks on immediate rivals and neighbours in Catalonia. The *sirventes* may date from the period he is thought to have spent in exile in Aquitaine (*c.*1175), which could make it a parody of the songs circulating in Occitania in the third quarter of the twelfth century, both sacred and secular. Interestingly, the Saint-Martial tropers BN lat. 1138 and 1338 are a single eleventh-century compilation of sequences signed by a certain Rotgerius, which Guido Maria Dreves entitled the *Sequentiarum Rotgeri* (*AH*, vii. 4–9).

'Un trichaire' has a basic three-line versicle structure, in a feminine rhyme form, with additional lines appended after the third versicle, which creates a long stanza with a rhythm different from that of the corpus under discussion. Frank hesitates between classifying the piece as an eleven-line stanza structure (Frank, 8), or as an eight-line stanza (Frank, 5 n.); I have opted for the structure closest to the corpus under discussion: a a a a a a a a a a a/ 3'3'7'3'3'7'3'3'7'7'7'.

Guillem attacks Rogier primarily as a priest who may be a fraud, and who travels from one end of the Poitou-Aquitaine region to the other, taking care of his priestly appearance and role:

> Un trichaire
> pestre laire
> vol que chan, pus sui chantaire.
> Cossirair'e
> mal pessaire
> serai del chan tro l'esclaire.
> De Sensaire
> Tro Belcaire
> a sercat lo gualiaire,
> trichan cum fol prezicaire:
> facha s'a.l corona raire.
> (vv. 1–11)

[I wish to sing about a cheating, thieving priest, since I am a singer. I'll be worried and 'ill-thinking' about the song until I've brought it to light. From Sancerre to Beaucaire the trickster has travelled, cheating like a foolish preacher. He's had his tonsure shaved.]

In the next stanza, the priest is addressed directly as 'Rogier fraire/ colom vaire' [Rogier, brother, inconstant dove] (v. 13), as a coward, a disgrace to his father and a man commonly rumoured to be unwilling to serve God (vv. 15–22). The song then moves into a discussion of the priest's misbehaviour in terms of violent sexual imagery, much of which is heavily indebted to Marcabru and Guilhem IX, with its references to the sweetness of the *con* (v. 28). After breaking with his vows, Rogier's exertions nearly break his back: 'e.l con non cessa ni fina/ qu'en la ciutat peitavina/ se rompet foten l'esquina' [and the cunt neither stops nor finishes; in the city of Poitiers, he broke his back fucking] (vv. 31–3).

The song's concern is with Rogier's misuse of his religious position: 'Res aurana/ Dieus engana/ cum desfassa.l ley Romana' [This frivolous being tricks God as he plots to undo the law of Rome] (vv. 45–7), as it moves through various witnessed allegations, into the realm of comic exaggeration, as Rogier travels the world on his errant mission (vv. 56–66). The song ends with a stanza written in parodic Latin, describing Rogier's copulation; again, this is strongly reminiscent of Guilhem IX, especially the combination of references to pilgrimage with nonsense speech in 'Farai un vers pos mi sonelh' (*PC* 183, 12, Pasero, V). In its combination of ecclesiastical language with obscenity, it comes close to Peire Cardenal's *estribot* discussed in the Introduction. This stanza breaks with the rest of the song by using masculine rhyme, which not only makes it an example of the scheme 44844844888 at this moment, but also makes it a stanza transgressing against the order of a transgressive song:

> Sai venc savis
> colors blavis
> per saber quals es peitavis.
> Anc clerguavis
> ni gramavis,
> sarrazis ni almoravis,
> non donavis
> tals culavis
> desobre fort de cons cavis.
> Rogier, greu auretz bos avis
> si la colla no.us tol clavis.
> (vv. 67–77)

[A wise man came here, with pallid colours, to know which one is the man from Poitou. Never before has any cleric, nor any grammarian, nor Saracen nor Almoravid, given so many butt-thrusts against so many concave cunts. Rogier, you'll find it hard to get good advice if the noose doesn't take your key.]

This song appears to address a known model in Latin, or related to ecclesiastical chant, as well as the songs of Guilhem IX and Marcabru. The idea of recognizing the man from Poitou through this stanza would reinforce the suggestion that Guillem is consciously pastiching a recognized 'Poitevin' style. The basic structure is three-line versicles, broken by an additional two heptameter lines, while its content is about rupture at all levels, from ethics and rules to vows and the body itself. Rogier is depicted as an immoral priest who lies, commits incest and consorts with whores. The song ends by breaking with its own rhyme scheme and its language, with a macaronic *cobla*.

In the *Sequentiarum Rotgeri*, as in the other Saint-Martial tropers, a number of sequences use the form adopted by Guillem de Berguedà. For example, the short piece 'Veneranda' (*AH*, vii. 52) opens as follows:

1a	Veneranda die ista pax hominibus est data	1b	Et aeterna laetitia atque beata gloria

Guillem appears to have appropriated a corpus of songs that were, like Rogier himself, travelling around the region, and rewritten them with malicious intent. 'Un trichaire' serves as an interesting counterpoint to Peire d'Alvernha's song in that it pushes the tensions within itself, as a hypertext containing both obscene and serious models, to its limits. It is a song which does not attempt to compete with its model by rewriting its words, but which seeks to ruin it internally, by turning Rogier's every move into a travesty of his devotional role.

Guillem's parody is a compendium of reductive devices. It dehumanizes, exaggerates and defames its object, devoting much attention to his actions, appearance and the distortions of his body, until 'Rogier' becomes a monster. The song is a caricature which invites the listener to identify the 'Poitevin' at its close. Compared to this outrageous display of invective, Peire's recuperation of Marcabru's noisome seducer into a smug penitent seems to be suffering from 'colors blavis' indeed. The differences between the parodies by Peire d'Alvernha and Guillem de Berguedà illustrate a key question: Is a parodic text destined to be received as a work filled with reverence for its target, or as an example of subversive reduction? It may be argued that this, in the end, can only be decided with reference to the audience's expectations, which are, in themselves, subject to variance.

Notes to Chapter 4

1. Grivel, 'Le retournement parodique', 8–11; Golopentia-Eretescu, 'La parodie et la feinte', 38–9.
2. Lehmann, *Parodie im Mittelalter* 144–5; *Carmina Burana*, 156, stanza 6.
3. Gaunt, *Troubadours and Irony*, 58–9.
4. Meneghetti, 'Un stornello nunziante', 47–63. See also Harvey, *Troubadour Marcabru and Love*, 158–93.
5. Harvey, *Troubadour Marcabru and Love*, 52–3, 58.
6. Stevens, *Words and Music*, 307–12; Dronke, *Medieval Lyric*, 50–1.
7. Kendrick, 'Jongleur as Propagandist'; see also *Game of Love*, 15–20.
8. See Goddard, 'Early Troubadours', and Pfeffer, *Proverbs in Medieval Occitan Poetry*; Coleman, *Ancient and Medieval Memories*, 132–5.
9. Hutcheon, *A Theory of Parody*, 65; Genette, *Palimpsestes*, 41–2.
10. Leslie T. Topsfield, *Troubadours and Love* (Cambridge: Cambridge University Press, 1975), 187–9; Dmitri Scheludko, 'Über die reliogiöse Lyrik der Troubadours', *Neuphilologische Mitteilungen* 38 (1937), 224–50.
11. Geneviève Hasenohr, 'La prédication aux fidèles dans la première moitié du XIIe siècle; L'enseignement des sermons "limousins"', *Romania* 116 (1998), 34–67 (53).
12. Hasenohr, 'La prédication aux fidèles', 58–65.
13. William D. Paden, '*De monachis rithmos facientibus*: Hélinant of Froidmont, Bertran de Born and the Cistercian General Chapter of 1199', *Speculum* 55 (1980), 669–85.
14. Meneghetti, 'Un stornello nunciante', 47–50.
15. Saffioti, *I Giullari in Italia*, 65–76 (68).
16. Saffioti, *I Giullari in Italia*, 65, 79.
17. Paterson, *Troubadours and Eloquence*, 77–83.
18. Topsfield, *Troubadours and Love*, 173–8.
19. Gaunt, *Troubadours and Irony*, 114–20.
20. Gaunt, *Troubadours and Irony*, 106–10, Topsfield, *Troubadours and Love*, 178–9.
21. See Roncaglia, 'Lo *gap* di Marcabru', 62.
22. Text from Frede Jensen, *Provençal Philology and the Poetry of Guillaume de Poitiers* (Odense: Odense University Press, 1983).
23. Amy Richlin, *The Garden of Priapus: Sexuality and Aggression in Roman Humour* (New Haven: Yale University Press, 1983), 65–7.
24. See Rose, *Parody*, 127.
25. Aniello Fratti, 'Un probabile caso di adattamento redazionale diacronico: la canzone-sirventese "Be m'es plazen" (*PC* 232, 10) di Peire d'Alvernhe', *Studi Mediolatini e Volgari* 39 (1993), 33–55; Giulio Bertoni, *Il canzionere provenzale di Bernart Amoros (Complemento Càmpori)* (Freiburg: Gschwend, 1911); for *z*, V. de Bartholomæis, 'Avanzi di un canzionere provenzale del secolo XIII', *Studi Romanzi* 12 (1915), 139–86; for *m*, A. Monteverdi, 'Pier d'Alvernia nel foglio superstite di un canzionere provenzale del duecento', *Studi Medievali* 12 (1939), 133–59.

26. Fratti, 'Un probabile caso', 34–8.
27. Antoine Tavera, 'Le congé de Peire d'Auvergne: un problème d'édition', in *Actes du Ve Congrès international de langue et de littérature d'oc et d'études franco-provençales, Nice, 6–12 septembre 1967*, ed. Gérard Miognet and Roger Lassalle (Paris: Les Belles Lettres, 1974), 444–56; Fratti, 'Un probabile caso', 34–9.
28. Fratti, 'Un probabile caso', 42–7.
29. Coleman, *Ancient and Medieval Memories*, 175–86; Paden, '*De monachis rithmos facientibus*'.
30. Aurelio Roncaglia, 'Riflessi di posizioni cistercensi nella poesia del XII secolo: Discussione sui fondamenti religiosi del "trobar naturau" di Marcabruno', *I Cisterciensi e il lazio: Atti delle giornate di studio dell'Instituto di Stori dell'Arte dell'Università di Roma, 17–22 maggio 1977* (Rome, 1978), 11–22 (13).
31. Coleman, *Ancient and Medieval Memories*, 181–5.
32. Coleman, *Ancient and Medieval Memories*, 184, citing the short version of *De conversione ad clericos*, intended for Parisian students, XIII, 25.
33. Caroline Walker Bynum, *Jesus as Mother: Studies in the Spirituality of the High Middle Ages* (Berkeley: University of California Press, 1982), 69–74.
34. Coleman, *Ancient and Medieval Memories*, 173–4, citing Berengarius's letter to Bernard, *PL* 178, col. 1857.
35. Gaunt, *Troubadours and Irony*, 114–20.
36. Bynum, *Jesus as Mother*, 127–8.

CHAPTER 5

❖

Between Preacher and Jester: Singing a Sermon

This chapter will open with a rapid analogy with modern concerns, citing a comic performer's view of her own, and others', parodic work: 'It wasn't so much whether your material was political or not; it could be and then again it may not be. That didn't seem to matter. It was the cleverness of it that mattered most, and people like [Jeremy] Hardy have said, and people have said of him, it's a good job he's good [...] because the audience actually don't like what he's saying. They just like the way that he says it.'[1] In an article about the stand-up woman comedian Jo Brand, Stephen Wagg proposes that the audience's own reception of political material may not be conditioned by its own ideological agreement or disapproval, but rather by its appreciation of the performer's skill. Wagg narrates the varied reactions to Brand's provocative comic persona, and concludes that the only consensus is that Brand's aggression inspires strong reactions to her act but not to the ideological content of her jokes, which are often politically committed. Brand herself is said to have honed her act from a play on her unconventional looks into a coherent persona which can sustain extended performances on television as well as in writing. For Wagg, this persona is based on her combination of overweight appearance and sexual banter, and builds on an important feature of contemporary British culture, that of the construction of women's identity in terms of body weight and aggression, which may reveal tensions in popular culture that other comedians or commentators, by virtue of being less immediately 'transgressive', cannot.

He adds that Ben Elton, a stand-up comedian with strong political commitment, has proved unpopular with some audiences because they resent the assumptions they read into his persona, which marries 'a kind of market trader type' with 'fairly proselytizing material':

'people became uncomfortable, not because they didn't agree with the substance but because they didn't like the manner in which it came at them'. In Elton's case, according to Wagg, the persona alienates the audience from material it is, in theory, prepared to accept. So performers of transgressive jokes, such as Jeremy Hardy, may be accepted despite disagreeable material, whereas others, such as Elton, may find that an unpleasant persona will negate the didactic message they seek to transmit.

In the context of British society at the turn of the twentieth century, such questions are important because of the political role assumed by mainstream comedians. The frequency with which stand-up comedians, many of whom are not associated with politicized material, are featured in relation to political affairs prompts Wagg to suggest that 'Comedians, increasingly, define us to ourselves'. This development may be similar to the use of court jesters in the medieval court as a regulatory mechanism, within which the fool acts as 'everyman' or the reverse image of the ruler; but this association of professional entertainers with mainstream media acceptability suggests that the material treated by these performers is assumed to be acceptable to a wide audience: it articulates orthodox opinions, which are generally identified as liberal; the participation of a professional clown in a political debate is not perceived as invalidating the seriousness of the discussion itself.

I would argue that this phenomenon is not purely modern, but the product of parodic strategies elaborated long before, given increased visibility by what Eco has termed the 'carnivalization of culture'.[2] This would emphasize the similarities between such a desacralization of political discourse and the secularization of sacred material in the medieval society under discussion. To have your society or culture defined by the words of a licensed entertainer is only a short jump away from two parallel and not necessarily incompatible genres, the jester's mockery and the preacher's invective. Political material in the medieval context may be understood in terms of religious moralizing, which had the explicit agenda of defining Christian society to itself. Given this situation, it should come as no surprise to see the chain of parodies examined in this study close not on a transgressive parody, but on a sermon.

The marriage of parodic form with proselytizing content may not be so startling after all, once the parallels between the licensed critic and the licensed fool are examined. In parodic texts, recuperation may be inscribed from the start. It follows that Peire Cardenal's sermons may contain within them both the serious preacher and the voices of his satirical predecessors.

Preachers were forced to be entertaining, and would have resorted to comic effects; they would have cultivated a strong persona. Meanwhile, the cultivation of personae for performance has long been traced in the troubadour corpus. While the *vidas* may preserve echoes of the poets' constructed rather than biographical selves, certain key texts provide fragmentary evidence for the self-presentation of troubadours when performing their songs. Peire d'Alvernha's 'poet's gallery' (*PC* 323, 11, Del Monte, XII) gives a thumbnail sketch of various troubadours which may indicate how they appeared or acted before their audience.[3] The Monk of Montaudon's *contrafactum* (*c.*1195) of this piece, 'Pos Peire d'Alvernh'a cantat' (*PC* 305, 16, Routledge, XVIII), gives details about the physical posture of some performers. Intriguingly, Peire Laroqua (only in *M*) seems to be credited with a particular style of performance for satirical material:

> Peires Laroqu'es le qinces,
> uns cavalliers de Cardenes,
> qe chanta mout nesciamen;
> e qan di vers ni serventes,
> diriatz qe febres l'a pres;
> aissi vai son cap secoden.
>
> (vv. 91–6)

[Peire Laroqua is the fifteenth, a knight of the Cardenès who sings in a very stupid way, and when he recites *vers* or *sirventes*, you would think a fever had taken hold of him, he shakes his head so.]

This seems to be confirmed by the rejected *cobla* about Guilhem de Ribas. In *ACDaIKLa*[1], the third line of the strophe says he 'canta sos vers raucamen' (he sings his *vers* hoarsely), whereas the same line in *R* states he 'canta volontiers non gen' (he sings not well, willingly). By way of comparison, the two troubadours cited by the Monk in terms of their performance of *cansos* are both credited with permanently weeping eyes (vv. 18, 59–60), while the criticism of Tremoleta's combination of dyed hair and strange posture seem to suggest that his 'cantars [...] de nien' (v. 51) is more about seduction than moralizing.[4]

Another source for this diversity of performance styles is to be found in the opening of a song by Uc de Lescura.[5] Borrowing the form from a poem by Peire Vidal, he has also envisaged its reception in terms of a number of other rivals:

De motz ricos no tem Peire Vidal
ni.NAlbertet de sa votz a ben dir
ni.NPerdigon de greu sonet bastir,
ni.NPegulhan de chansos metr' en sal,
ni de gabar sos chans N'Arnaut Romieu
ni de lausar Fonsalada son fieu,
ni.NPelardit de contrafar la gen,
ni.NGualaubet de viular coyndamen.
(vv. 1–8)

[For his noble words I do not fear Peire Vidal, nor do I fear Albertet for his voice when reciting well, nor Perdigon for his construction of a difficult melody, nor Peguilhan for adding savour to his *cansos*, nor Arnaut Romieu for bragging in his songs, nor Fonsalada for praising his fief, nor Pelardit for mimicking people, nor Gualaubet for playing the *vielle* elegantly.]

For Uc de Lescura, *trobar* is not simply a question of acknowledging the formal and stylistic debt of his *contrafactum*. It also involves a dynamic relationship with the beauty of Albertet's voice, and the differing styles of performance implied by Aimeric de Peguilhan's 'spicing up' of his lyrics, compared to Arnaut Romieu's hearty renditions, and Elias Fonsalada's more decorous performances. Pelardit and Gualaubet, who are probably *joglars*, are credited with the cultivation of specific skills. The distinction made here between 'gabar' and 'lausar' implies, once again, a difference in performance styles related to genre. Moreover, it is unsurprising to find Uc challenging Peire Vidal, whose songs and *vida* point to an extravagant persona cultivated through clowning, costume and performance (*BS*, LVII).

Performance was also essential to the success of a preacher. Peire Cardenal's attack on the Dominican order describes them first as expert performers of their sermons:

Ab votz d'angel, lengu'esperta, non bleza,
Ab motz sotils, plans plus c'obra d'engles,
Ben assetatz, ben ditz e sens repreza,
Miels escoutatz, ses tossir, que apres,
Ab plans, sanglotz, mostran la via
De Jhesu-Crist, que quex deuria
Tener, com el per nos la volc tener.
Van prezican com puescam Dieu vezer.
(*PC* 335, 1, XXVIII, vv. 1–8)

[With an angel's voice and an expert tongue that doesn't lisp, with subtle words, smoother than English cloth, well placed, well spoken, without repetition, better listened to without coughing, than learned, with weeping and sobbing they show the way of Jesus Christ, that everyone should follow, as He wished to follow it for us. They go preaching how we might see God.]

This powerful sketch of the Dominicans at work points to the source of their effective oratory: they speak smoothly and continuously, demanding silence of their audience, and seem to rely more on emotional impact than intellectual effect; this at least seems to be the import of the comment that their words are 'miels escoutatz [...] que apres'. Peire depicts their inquisitorial activity in their *cort* as the product of their inability to observe the rule of silence instituted by the early monastic orders (vv. 25–32). There is a hint in this song that the Dominicans present a considerable threat to the secular entertainer.

Given these factors, it should come as less of a surprise to see the correlation between Guerau de Cabrera and Guiraut de Calanson's admonitions to their *joglars*, and the opening of Peire Cardenal's versified sermon 'Predicator'. Both distinguished by their use of the *vielle*, the performers addressed by one text and constructed by the other are both anxious to entertain their audience, to keep their attention and to emphasize their point over an extended performance. Whereas Guiraut's poem seems to depend on the success of its invective as comic boast, the sermon seeks to present what may be described as 'fairly proselytizing material' in an attractive manner. Both texts claim to wish to correct their addressees, but the step from the one-sided mockery of a silent *joglar* to the admonition of the congregation of a sermon demands a degree of contextualization before it may be adequately understood.

Peire Cardenal's sermon 'Predicator' is exceptional in the chain of parodies studied here by virtue of its explicitly devotional content. Manuscript *I* rubricates 'Predicator' as 'sermon VII', which implies that Peire composed at least six similar texts. Those extant poems include another sermon, 'Jhesu Crist' (*PC* 335, 27, LV), which will be examined later, a moralizing fable, 'Una ciutatz fo, no sai cals' (no *PC* number, Lavaud, LXXX), and several devotional songs, including the homiletic crusade song 'Dels quatre caps que a la cros' (*PC* 335, 15, XXX). Peire's monologue by an ointment-seller 'Sel que fes' (*PC* 335, 14, LXXI) may be connected to the tradition of the ointment-seller's speech in Resurrection plays, but this is merely a hypothesis. As it stands, the text has no devotional content.

Peire Cardenal's versified sermons are similar to versified sermons found in the Anglo-Norman corpus, as well as to extant didactic texts in Occitan. Its closest models, however, lie in the surviving evidence of vernacularized liturgical and related texts in Occitan. A number of vernacular devotional and didactic texts seem to stem from a lively cultivation of religious culture. Cerverí de Girona's *Sermo* and *Oració de tot dia* reflect a secular form of piety in thirteenth-century Catalan courts, as do the devotional songs to the Virgin from the same period by Guiraut Riquier, Falquet de Romans, Folquet de Marseilles and other poets. Peire de Courbian, for example, justifies his use of the vernacular as an act of faith:

> Domna, dels angels regina,
> esperansa dels crezens,
> segon que.m comanda sens,
> chan de vos lenga romana;
> quar nulhs hom justz ni peccaire
> de vos lauzar no.s deu traire,
> cum sos sens mielhs l'aparelha,
> romans o lenga latina.[6]
>
> (vv. 1–8)

[Lady, queen of the angels, hope of believers, as sense commands me to, I sing of you in the Romance tongue; for no man, just or sinful, should keep from praising you as his sense best equips him to do, in Romance or in the Latin tongue.]

Other devotional texts, such as the anonymous *Arlabecca* or Folquet de Lunel's *Roman de mondana vida*, adopt a preacher's voice to construct what are effectively sermons in verse.[7] It is very likely that devotional song was performed in courtly settings. The diffusion of these texts within troubadour *chansonniers* points to the popularity among the laity of devotional material. Sources external to the *chansonnier* corpus, however, may yield a better picture of devotional activity in the vernacular outside court circles.

Raimon de Castelnou's *Doctrinal* is preserved in a codex compiled by Peyre de Serras in the mid-fourteenth century, near Avignon, which includes recipes, accounts and a selection of devotional texts in the vernacular, probably intended for private use.[8] These texts show the profound influence of vernacularization on the devotional practices of the laity, including translations and paraphrases of the *Pater*, the *Ave Maria* and the *Credo*, hagiographies and a version of the Marian *Gardacors*. While Peyre's accounts date his activities to *c.*1347–57, certain texts, such as the *vita* of St Margaret, dated 1 May 1284, appear to have been copied earlier, and the *Doctrinal*, as was stated earlier, is apparently datable to *c.*1229.

Certain pieces in Peyre de Serras's collection are destined for teaching purposes, and show evidence of wide diffusion. The extract from the Dominican *Somme le Roi* (1279) is an Occitan translation belonging to a separate tradition from the three surviving Occitan versions of this text. The versified paraphrase of the *Credo* is a 42-line text which states that, rather than serving as a prop for the acquisition of Church Latin, it is composed for the benefit of those who may speak the text in the vernacular. This manuscript shows the imbrication of devotional and vernacular material.

Another manuscript composed in the region of Apt by an anonymous Franciscan between *c.*1317 and *c.*1369 contains Occitan translations and paraphrases of the penitential psalms and of the litanies of the saints.[9] Chabaneau notes the existence of a parallel paraphrase of the penitential psalms and other vernacularized texts.[10] These texts, which may be from an earlier date, seem to reflect usage not condoned by the Church. The penitential psalms appear to have been performed door-to-door in versified translation until the sixteenth century, and Chabaneau suggests that texts such as the translation of Psalm 108 were used in domestic rituals for cursing enemies,[11] but these pieces also illustrate the catechetical work of parish priests and friars in Occitan regions in this period.

The Franciscan's poems are a transitional stage between devotional vernacular texts and troubadour song. The most common metrical scheme used in these pieces is the octosyllabic quatrain, in the forms aabb or abab, with occasional examples of more sophisticated structures, such as the version of Psalm 1 in the form ababccd 66'66'444'.[12] The texts vary from transliteration to free adaptation; for example, the translation of Psalm 101:10 (*NEB* 102:9), 'Quia cinerem tanquam panem manducabam, Et potum meum cum fletu miscebam' [I have eaten ashes for bread and mingled tears with my drink], attempts a line-by-line rendering of the text, while the paraphrase alters the meaning, opening each quatrain with an apostrophe to Christ and enacting a ritualized penitential gesture. The translation reads: 'Car senre[s] aysin con pan manjava/ E lo mieu beure an plor mesclava' [For I ate ashes with bread, and mingled my drink with tears] (vv. 33–4). The paraphrase gives the following version of the Biblical text:

> Ihesus, pan de penalitat
> A[d] dolor per me has minyat,
> Begut potatge fort amar,
> preg te volhas me perdonar.
> (vv. 347–50)

[Jesus, you have eaten the bread of penitence in pain, for my sake, and drunk bitter beverage; I pray for you to forgive me.]

The Franciscan of Apt also wrote down vernacularized litanies, in sixty-eight *coblas* with an alternation of masculine and feminine rhymes: ababcbcb, 7'77'77'77'7:[13]

> Las letanias romansadas
> Totz homs [a]ysi trobara,
> Las cals a per sertz dechadas,
> Per endreysar totz cor [va],
> Un endigne fil e frayre
> De sant Frances totz de pla[n],
> E qui vol las volra retrayre
> En aysin comensara.
> (vv. 1–8)

[The litanies put into the Romance language will be found here by all men, which were made, in order to set straight all hearts, by an unworthy son and brother of St Francis, simply; and whoever wishes to present them will begin like this.]

The second stanza enacts the despair of the penitent—presumably not that of the author, but of the person who has chosen to perform the litanies as their speaker:

> Heu, forfacha creatura
> C'ay laisatz mon creator,
> E segut se[ne]s mesura
> Del mont la[s] falsa[s] honor[s].
> (vv. 9–12)

[Alas, wretched creature! I have abandoned my Creator, and followed, immoderately, the false honours of the world.]

While this song plays on penitential imagery and Scriptural allusions it may have borrowed from Latin sources, it is striking to find echoes of vernacular lyric. The Franciscan's text displays a characteristic intermingling of emotivity, personal address and versification which provides a clear analogue to the sermons attributed to Peire Cardenal.

Connections between Franciscans and the troubadour lyric are rare but attested; one example is the song to Mary attributed to a 'Fraire Menor' discussed in a previous chapter. Another is the career, contemporary with the activity of the Franciscan of Apt and Peyre de Serras, of Raimon de Cornet. This poet, who flourished between *c.*1320 and *c.*1349, claimed to have been a spiritual Franciscan for less than a year around 1325–6.[14] Raimon's varied poetic output has been interpreted and dated in terms of its mixture of secular and spiritual elements, as well as the evidence that he continued to compose poetry after his entry into the Cistercian order. According to René Nelli, Raimon de Cornet continued to articulate ideas associated with the beghards in the 1330s, producing hermetic spiritual poems that combine secular motifs with Marian symbols.[15] There are some indications that the transmission of the poems of Raimon de Cornet may have been conflated with that of songs by Peire Cardenal.[16] However, Raimon was active at a later date, in a social context that had altered quite radically; Toulouse by the 1330s was a university city under close ecclesiastical control, engaged in intensive interaction with the papacy in Avignon. It is perhaps inevitable that the poems of this period should bear the imprint of a changed society.

The sermons of Peire Cardenal are unusual in that they appear to be the work of a secular figure, addressing a predominantly secular audience in his familiar—anti-clerical—persona. The sermon 'Jhesus Cristz, nostre salvaire' (*PC* 335, 27, LV) is in the metre found in other vernacularized texts, aaab, 7'7'7'7 with a fixed b-rhyme in '-en'. It is 329 lines long and stages a sweeping denunciation of a wide range of sins. The sermon does not present a penitential speaker, nor any evidence of an individualized voice; it opens on a statement that it is 'cortezia' to emulate Christ in saving others (vv. 1–16), and seems to present the sermon as a charitable deed:

Per que hom que salut voilha
De salut faire no.s tuoilha;
E cora que salut cuoilha
Semen la premieiramen.

(vv. 21–4)

[For the man who wishes to be saved doesn't hold back from saving others; and for every moment he gathers salvation, let him sow it first.]

From stanza 8, the text directly addresses those it perceives as sinners, either through apostrophe, 'Aus tu, que as draps e peilhas' (Do you hear, who have cloth and clothing?) (v. 33), or with sententious statements, 'Ja neguns homs que Dieu creza / Non amassara riqueza' (No man who believes in God will ever gather wealth). It appears to be the product of an impersonal and stern speaker who aims to ensure the mutual vigilance of secular 'neighbours':

Dieus comanda c'on entenda
Sos comans e que.l aprenda,
E totz sos vezis reprenda
Can n'aura conoissamen.
(vv. 65–8)

[God commands that people should listen to his commandments and learn them, and that one should upbraid one's neighbours when one hears of their behaviour.]

The sermon is a satire on the estates, addressing priests (vv. 81–4), warmongering prelates (vv. 89–92), those who judge or excommunicate abusively (vv. 101–20), and others; it then moves on to secular figures such as physicians (vv. 125–32) and labourers (vv. 237–40). The text moves from the recommendation of charitable acts to an exhortation to penitence (vv. 281–304). The speaker appears to associate himself with the parish priest, as well as with a general struggle against incorrect doctrinal teaching:

Dieus non vol sias toleire
E vol crezas ton preveire
Que.ils bens que.t mostra deus creire
Senes tot corrompemen.
(vv. 305–8)

[God does not wish you to be a thief, and wants you to believe your priest, for you must believe in the good things he shows you, without any corrupting of them.]

At the close of this long harangue, the speaker invites his audience to join him in prayer, hoping they shall all be saved from 'horrible, stinking Hell' (vv. 317–29).

Compared to this forbidding text, the sermon 'Predicator' shows signs of a more ingratiating rhetorical approach, and seems to place its speaker centre-stage, without, however, adopting the penitential self-abasement of either Raimon de Castelnou or the Apt Franciscan. It is shorter, in thirty-one stanzas with a constant b-rhyme in '-ar', and aims to advise rather than exhort. It is interesting for its painstaking, and lengthy, justification of its preaching enterprise, which produces a preamble almost a third of the length of the entire piece, and seems to indicate a defensive approach towards a reluctant audience. The very small number of variants in the four extant versions of this text indicate that it circulated in a stable written form, with no permutation of stanzas. 'Jhesus Cristz', on the other hand, has an unstable manuscript tradition: extant in four manuscripts, it shows evidence of omissions and restructuring. Performers may have made cuts in the text.

The first statement in the song is that a good 'predicator' should preach by example (vv. 1–12). The next stanza, as was said in Chapter 1 above, attempts to persuade its audience to listen patiently, by promising them a more attractive song later. Not content with this conditional promise, he goes on to promise this will not be a Hellfire sermon, and that his aim is not to upset them:

> Ieu ai en cor
> Que, per demor
> Ni per rire ni per jogar,
> No.us diga huei
> Mal ni enuei,
> De guiza que.us deia pezar.
> (vv. 19–24)

[I have the intention, at my own leisure, neither in laughter nor in sport, to tell you today nothing bad or annoying that might make you downcast.]

The speaker insists that he merely wishes to pass on useful and improving knowledge (vv. 25–7) and begs his listeners not to turn on him for criticizing their mores: 'E s'ie.us repren/ Adrechamen/ No m'o deves a mal tornar' [And if I criticize you as I should, you mustn't see this as a bad thing on my part] (vv. 28–30). This plea is underlined by an *exemplum*: a man who catches a child throwing stones will beat it more readily if it is his own son, than if it is someone else's (vv. 31–6). It follows that the preacher's sharpest comments should be taken as a demonstration of his love, but the speaker doubts if this will happen: he is tired of thankless tasks, illustrating this with the unpleasant image of trying to comb a man suffering from ringworm (vv. 37–42). Indeed, he is already exasperated by his audience's heedlessness of his words:

Con plus vos dic
E plus m'afic
En vos, castian, enseinhar,
Vos fest pejor:
Per c'ai paor
Que m'en covenga a laisar.
(vv. 43–8)

[The more I speak, the more I strive to instruct you with chastisement, the worse you act; that's why I'm afraid I may have to give up.]

This complaint is illustrated by the Biblical image of the seeds sown on barren or desert ground (vv. 49–54), and a comparison of the audience with a fine vessel needing to be emptied of sin before it can be filled with goodness (vv. 55–72). The speaker's other target is his listeners' 'mala fe' (v. 73) which leads to mutual suspicion.

His stated aim is to teach the audience to become good examples of 'baro' (vv. 79–84). This does not mean that the sermon is addressing an audience of the upper nobility, for, as the preacher goes on to say, wealth and standing do not make the distinction between a 'cusson' (a churl) and a 'baro' (vv. 85–102). However, the repeated comments about warfare and the use of such objects as costly vessels, rich clothing (vv. 97–102) and shields (v. 96) indicate a knightly audience. In line 119, the speaker describes his listeners as 'manen', wealthy people. The sermon's focus on issues of military behaviour places it in contrast to 'Jhesus Cristz' and its emphasis on the behaviour of prelates and clerks. The sermon defines the 'baro' as a man of virtue: 'Sol car es pros/ E.il plas razos/ Lo deu hom baron apellar' [Simply because he is worthy, and a friend to reason, one should call him a baron] (vv. 106–8).

The sermon's list of precepts for the good conduct of a wealthy man in society eschews exhortations to penance. It seems to promote an ethos of charitable good conduct and justice, condemning repressive measures (vv. 115–32), but also to insert unexpected precepts:

Perdonatz leu
Vengatz vos greu,
E non vos cal cheira portar;
Amas amix
E enemix,
E no.us cal anar outra mar.
(vv. 133–8)

[Be swift to forgive and slow to avenge yourself, and do not wear a hairshirt. Love your friends and your enemies, and do not go *Outremer*.]

This last stanza could be interpreted as evidence of the disenchantment of the Occitan population with the notion of crusading after the Albigensian wars; it could be argued, however, that for a sermon to the wealthy warrior class to advise its members against mortification of the flesh, crusade or pilgrimage shows a wish to please them that is, at best, contrary to penitential preaching.[17] As Michel Zink notes, the examination of contrition and repentance and the exhortation towards penitence were crucial elements of much vernacular preaching in the twelfth and thirteenth centuries. Occitan homilies urge the listener to repent in this life 'in cinere et cilicio' in order to alleviate the punishments to come.[18] The speaker of the sermon 'Predicator' seems to be adopting an unusual position with respect to ecclesiastical preachers of the time.

The preacher summarizes the acquistion of *valor* [worth] through a metaphor related to the costly vessels, clothes and charitable deeds he has described, rather than penance; the good man will not abase himself or others in pursuit of worth, but will purchase it through his own refinement of the self, and his practice of moderation. He will effectively acquire *valor* through his own enrichment and his social activity:

Car hom non a
Valor en va
Ans la li coven a comprar;
De son aver
De son saber,
De son conseil, de son parlar.
(vv. 145–50)

[For no man has *valor* for free; instead, he should purchase it with his wealth, with his knowledge, with his advice, with his speech.]

This passage implies a context more typical of a town than of a court, with its emphasis on the interaction of peers in an economy of exchange and mutual benefit, where the poor are equally present and active. Harmonious interaction and conduct appears to be the goal of the preacher's precepts; to please God, and to be 'pros e cortes', is to do nothing displeasing and to follow the appropriate rules (vv. 157–62). To be 'hom leials' (v. 164) is simply to follow the Law: 'Qui la lei cre/ E la lei te/ E segon la lei vol obrar' [Whoever believes in the Law, and upholds the Law, and wishes to work according to the Law] (vv. 166–8). The man who can do this will go with God (vv. 169–74) and be fully rewarded and guarded by the Law he protects, 'Cascuns er garda de son par' [each one will be the guardian of his peer] (v. 180). The sermon closes with the proverbial message that good deeds will be rewarded, and a command to watch over and improve the self:

> Et ab aitan,
> Anem enan
> E laissen lo sermon estar;
> Qui ben fara
> Ben trobara;
> Per c'om di: que cascuns si gar.
> (vv. 181–6)

[And on this note let's go our way, and let the sermon stand; whoever does good, will find good. Which is why it is said: Let each man look to himself.]

In its emphasis on the cultivation of controlled self-sufficiency, and a practice of charitable behaviour that aims to maintain the stability of the individual and of his social network, this song is more akin to a courtly *ensenhamen* than to a sermon in the penitential mould of the other texts cited in this study. Indeed, it is strikingly unconcerned with Christian terminology or doctrine, with a single reference to baptism in the preamble (v. 105), and no mention of either Christ or the Virgin. Instead, all elements of doctrine are left undefined, under the term 'la lei' and references to 'Dieus' alone. The focus is on pragmatic social interaction, and the avoidance of conflict and suffering. The text may open with a description of a good preacher, but it labels itself a *casteis* (chastisement) (vv. 39, 45) and seeks neither to exhort nor to convert, but to instruct. Its avoidance of doctrinal issues may indicate that the audience it addresses is both secular and doctrinally mixed, and that the speaker, in keeping with his reassuring opening, does not wish to address questions of orthodoxy and heresy that might alienate some of his listeners.

Peire Cardenal's sermons are not typical, in that they do not use the fashionable structures and rhetoric of the period. The review of the estates in 'Jhesus Cristz', for example, is a rare device in vernacular sermons; Zink notes only one example addressed to a lay audience, as well as the sermons of St Bernard, who distinguishes between three estates: prelates, monks and laymen.[19] The focus of 'Predicator' on the pragmatic virtues of nobility, on the other hand, is close to the attitudes espoused by some, such as the *prédicateur de l'Arsenal*, and the Tortosa preacher, who are more closely connected to their lay audience.[20] A good example of a contemporary sermon composed according to the rules is Cerverí de Girona's *Sermo* (de Riquer, 118), which follows the fashionable tripartite model also known as the 'plan victorin'.[21] Rubricated as a text composed in response to a challenge posed by a Franciscan friar, it opens with the theme, 'Surgens Deus mane' (vv. 10–13), interpreted literally (the first level) as the specific morning duties of merchants, labourers and pilgrims (vv. 14–39). As the second level of interpretation, Cerverí gives an allegorical reading of Christ's three actions of early rising; these are applied to the literal level (vv. 40–126), and produce the third level of interpretation, an anagogical statement listing three reasons why the audience should rise early (vv. 127–59). Additional elements are added, but the body of the text is coherent and summarized in conclusion (vv. 182–9). Miriam Cabré's study of Cerverí emphasizes the extent to which the Catalan troubadour made use of preaching devices,[22] which appear in his opening prayer for clear oratory and a comprehending audience (vv. 1–9). The presentation of the speaker is deferentially understated, and interventions throughout the sermon privilege the content over its performer, in keeping with the advice of thirteenth-century writers, and with the late date of this text, which de Riquer dates *c.*1250-*c.*1280.[23]

The content of 'Predicator' appears to be in line with the general ethos of moralizing in the vernacular sermon corpus, which Michel Zink reads as more pragmatic than its Latin counterpart. This 'morale de l'acte plutôt que de l'intention'[24] is explained as the need to provide uneducated listeners with simple rules they could learn and apply rather than theological arguments which could prove confusing. He also refers to the thirteenth-century focus on the sacrament itself as an efficacious act, surmising that this, again, would discourage introspection in the listener. However, neither sermon appears to be interested in the sacraments, nor in confession. In fact, both texts are closer to a *casteis*, as the use of the term in 'Predicator' indicates.

The term *castiar* has a specific usage in troubadour poetry. Derived from the Latin *castigare*, it may be translated as admonition, reproof or physical chastisement. A translation of Paul's Epistle to Titus, 3:10, states: 'l'ome erege apres la primeira e la segonda castiansa esquiva' [when dealing with a heretic, after the first and second admonition, avoid him].[25] Defined in terms of teaching and upbraiding, *castiar* was presented as a general obligation, as one of the seven 'obras de misericordia espiritals', in a twelfth-century manuscript from Saint-Martial-de-Limoges:[26]

donar bon conseil
chastiar celui que fai mal
conortar ome en sa tribulacio
perdonar celui que fay mal o lo di
sufrir ome rebelle e malfasedor
orar e prejar Deu per lui
esenhar e endoctrinar ome que no sap.

[To give good advice; to upbraid the one who does wrong; to comfort a man in his suffering; to forgive the one who does evil, or speaks it; to suffer a rebellious or wicked man; to pray and implore God on his behalf; to teach and indoctrinate the one who does not know.]

At least four of these duties involve persuasive speech, and are reflected in the admonitions of 'Predicator' to persist in correcting others through speech, as well as the identification of *castiar* with beating a child or, more unusually, with combing a diseased man. These moral obligations are applicable both to clerks and the laity, who are instructed to advise, teach, indoctrinate and admonish or control those who are perceived to be transgressors. While this may be equated with loving counsel, for example in the *cansos* of Giraut de Bornelh, it also has a sense of moral admonition, especially in satirical poetry.[27]

Ben deu hom chastian dire
Al sieu amic humilmen
Son bon conseil drechamen,
Qan el fa desmezuransa,
Si tot no.ill platz c'om ho dia;
(*PC* 242, 18a, Sharman, II, vv. 1–4)

[A man should indeed give his friend his good counsel as admonition, directly and with humility, when he acts immoderately, even if he doesn't like what he is told.]

So when Guilhem IX warns his listeners about the fate of 'sel qui no.n volra.n creire mos casteis' (v. 13), and Peire Cardenal and Peire d'Alvernha both announce that they wish to 'castian enseinhar'

('Predicator', v. 45) and 'castiar' ('Be m'es plazen', v. 21) their audience, the reference is to a complex of admonitory and meliorative uses of language, doctrine and discipline which imply a key element of intentionality. In all cases, the idea of *castiar* is related both to criticism and to improvement of the listener via the text; it may also be intended to imply the improvement of the text itself. However, Marcabru's statement 'De nien sui chastiaire/ E de foudat sermonaire' [I am the upbraider of nothing, and the preacher of folly] (*PC* 293, 5, V, vv. 31–2) shows the ambiguity of the *casteis*; the deployment of rhetorical skills may slip from the speaker's control, and prove counterproductive. The lines above may be intepreted as 'I am the man who upbraids nothingness and folly' and as 'I am the man who preaches nothingness and folly'. The act of condemnation may be the promotion of the object of its speech, and admonition may produce the sin it castigates. Furthermore, a lay or wandering preacher in this period of the Middle Ages was suspect; as the *estribot* and other texts in this study have shown, the concern with false preachers, and those who teach inaccurate doctrine, was intense. This may explain, at least in part, the speaker's extended, and highly defensive, justification of his performance in the opening of 'Predicator'.

If Peire Cardenal's sermons are both accurately attributed to him, as is the *estribot*, it is tempting to read 'Predicator', with its stern warning that the only valid preacher is the one who sets the right example through his actions, as a response to the approach of Raimon de Castelnou in his *Doctrinal*. Specious references to 'bons clercs' and their teachings are implicitly rejected in favour of a pragmatic morality based on social action and the avoidance of doctrinal issues altogether, but modelled on the versified sermons associated with the friars. Peire's appropriation of the metrical structure used for a number of parodic texts seems to make sense if 'Predicator' is viewed as a devotional text composed in opposition to the vernacularized devotional material surrounding it, a corpus which 'Jhesus Cristz' emulates in its aaab octosyllabic form. The opposition of the author is signalled by the use of a metrical structure familiar in terms of its parodic function with respect to the sacred. Peire's work is only partly a recuperation *a lo divino* of the metrical structure; it also builds on its association with disruption, rupture and competition between texts.

This return to penitence is telling, in that it illustrates the oscillation between orthodoxy and secularization that characterizes the poetry of both Peire Cardenal and others; the dialogue between disruptive and corrective words shows the ambiguity, and the politically delicate positioning, of their words.

Peire's rhetorical approach is little different from that of other vernacular preachers active before 1215. The northern French bishop of Sens, Maurice de Sully (fl. *c.*1170), adopts an equally *ad hominem* tone in his vernacular sermons, despite his solid training in Victorine theology, in order to inspire his audience with the requisite penitence. Stephen Langton (fl. 1206–28) recommends the use of 'rude, rustic exhortation' for the laity.[28] The sermons produced by this troubadour differ in that the speaker is, at least ostensibly, a member of the laity with a critical view of the clergy; in turn, this appeals to questions of performance.

As the opening of this chapter showed, performance involves more than words and metrical structure. A few troubadours presented their staged identity as a bridge between spiritual and secular spheres. Most notable among this group was the Monk of Montaudon (fl. *c.*1191–*c.*1214), whose corpus of songs may provide clues for the possible literary role of parodic preaching. The Monk of Montaudon has not been identified; his *vida* (*BS* LXVI) states he was born a nobleman and was a monk in the monastery of Aurillac, a powerful Benedictine house. As prior of Montaudon, a small priory attached to Aurillac, the Monk composed topical *sirventes* and *coblas* that brought him gifts from neighbouring noblemen and enabled him to make improvements to his church. The Monk was granted permission to leave the cloister, and was ordered by the king of Aragon 'to eat meat, court women and compose and perform poetry' (*BS* LXVI, 10). His later career involved presiding over the poetic court of Le Puy and continued success at the royal court in Spain. Michael Routledge has suggested that this biography is based on material found in certain songs. It is more likely that the Monk, whose songs refer to noble figures in the Auvergne and Limousin, was involved in the circle of Richard I Lionheart and Dalfin d'Auvergne.[29]

The Monk's corpus of songs is varied. His *cansos* make no reference to his monastic status. The five satirical *enueg* and *plazer* are, again, addressed to an audience of Toulousain nobles, with few to no allusions to clerical matters. However, the *tensos* feature evidence of play on homiletic material. In their form, the songs are typical of the rest of the troubadour corpus. It is worth noting that the abbey of Aurillac is the source of some of the pieces in the Aquitainian chant repertory, and was one of the most influential religious houses in the region.[30]

In four texts, the Monk claims to have made a visit to Heaven, and to have engaged in dialogues with various divine figures. The *tenso* 'L'autrier fuy en Paradis' (*PC* 305, 12, XIII) narrates a dialogue between the Monk and God, in which the Monk is rebuked for his decision to return to his cloistered life. His rejection of a secular career has lost him the patronage of the nobility (vv. 9–16). God answers that the Monk would have been better placed continuing to perform outside the monastery than indulging in political struggles with his neighbours (vv. 17–24). When he protests that he was afraid that his composition of *coblas* and *cansos* would earn him divine punishment, he is told that on the contrary, his lack of loyalty to his secular patron has been a more serious transgression (vv. 25–40). This song seems to present a parodic vision of the spiritual estate, in which life within the cloister is interpreted as disloyalty to the interests of the outside world, as well as to those of the economic well-being of priories. It is set, if not composed, during the imprisonment of Richard I Lionheart (*c.*1191–3) (vv. 34–48), and may be interpreted as a comment on topical matters. The last stanza seems to warn its listeners that inactivity (religious contemplation) may produce political disaster: Acre may fall again to the Saracens.

The cycle of songs XIV, XV and XVI presents more traditional material. In 'Autra vetz fuy a parlemen' (*PC* 305, 7, XIV) and 'Quan tuit aquist clam foron fat' (*PC* 305, 11, XVI), the Monk witnesses a debate in Heaven between church statues (or images) and ladies, concerning the use of cosmetics. The statues complain that the paint intended for them has been made too expensive by women's use of it. 'Autra vetz fuy a parlemen' presents an increasingly obscene discussion of the role of sex and urine in the ageing process, during which the Monk claims he can never satisfy the appetite of women (v. 62). God condemns the use of cosmetics by living creatures, but the Monk supports it, and criticizes his interlocutor for having too high an opinion of himself (vv. 33–4). The second song is composed in a different metrical scheme, and presents the conclusion of the debate. After a fierce discussion between the statues and women, God proposes that women aged over 25 should be allowed to use make-up for twenty years. The statues wish for ten, but St Peter and St Leonard arbitrate, and decree that the use of cosmetics for fifteen years should be permitted. The song ends with a detailed enumeration of the cosmetics concerned, and the remark that women ignore the decree to this day.

The two songs are bridged by a further Heavenly dialogue (*PC* 305, 11, XV), in which St Julian-the-Hospitaller complains that he is no longer the object of the prayers of travellers hoping to find a welcoming hearth. This song becomes a list of regions in which the rules of hospitality are still observed, encompassing the Auvergne, the Languedoc, Provence and Catalonia.

The three songs are compiled as a cycle of three consecutive texts in several manuscripts,[31] which implies that they are intended to be performed together, possibly sequentially. The second and third piece are joined formally by a shared metrical scheme, aabab, 88484, which is unique to the Monk but similar to one used twice by Guilhem IX, aaabab, 888484 (Frank, 55) and attested in the Aquitainian repertoire (Paris BN lat. 3719, f. 42):

> Dizon las domnas qe cent anz
> lor fo donaz lo peinz enanz
>   que fos trobatz
> vouz deguns el mon paucs no granz;
>   et es vertatz.
>
> (Routledge, XVI, vv. 16–20)

[The ladies say that they were given the paint a hundred years before any images, big or small, were made in the world; and this is true.]

The Monk's heavenly excursions show strong similarities to certain *fabliaux*, in which peasants and *jongleurs* engage in scurrilous encounters with Heaven and Hell. However, the narrator and protagonist of these songs is a man endowed with the authority to visit Heaven, interact with the saints and receive orders directly from God. In such *fabliaux* as *Saint Pierre et le jongleur*, *Le Vilain qui conquist Paradis par plait* and *Du Pet au vilain*, the parodic treatment of spiritual material plays on the incongruity of flatulent peasants harrowing Hell, or St Peter playing at dice with minstrels.[32] Here, the monastic speaker is an onlooker for absurd behaviour on the part of statues and saints, incongruous only in his inability to make his own repentance acceptable to a divinity more interested in the welfare of kings. Furthermore, the treatment of God is highly irreverent, compared even to that of the fabliaux; He swears 'per m'amor' (v. 12), and is rebuked by the Monk for his pride, 'Senher, trop parlatz ricamen/ car vos sentetz en altura' [Lord, you speak too haughtily, for you feel yourself to be high-up] (XIV, vv. 33–4). He also admits to having little idea of women's sexual experience, a point on which the Monk is keen to enlighten him:

'Monge, penhers ab afachar
lor fai mainhs colps d'aval sofrir
e no.us pessetz ges que lur tir
quant hom las fai corbas estar?'

'Senhers, fuecs las puesca cremar;
qu'ieu non lur puesc lur traucs omplir,
ans, quan cug a riba venir—
adoncs me cove a nadar.'

(XIV, vv. 57–64)

['Monk, painting with cosmetics makes them endure many blows from beneath, and don't you think it might be tight for them when men make them stay bent over?'
'Lord, Hellfire can burn them, for I can never fill their holes, and when I think I've reached the riverbank—then I have to start swimming [again].']

The cycle of Heavenly dialogues is also closely connected to sermon material; sermons condemning the use of cosmetics by women are attested from an early period, and the narrative frame of these texts suggests an *exemplum* format. A preacher from northern France expresses his disapproval of women's vanity in terms that echo those of the Monk: 'Celes qui avec leur cols et leur cheveuls descuevrent et oignent leur sorcilz et vernicent leur faces come ymage [...] cestes sont fornaises ardanz de luxure et sont mariees au deable'.[33] God's arguments against the use of make-up by women are also drawn from firm moralizing ground: beauty cannot be assumed without divine permission (vv. 25–8) and the ageing process cannot be reversed (vv. 29–32).

The persona of the Monk of Montaudon may seem anomalous. He presents himself as an enthusiastic sinner, who has abandoned his vocation with glee, yet keeps his privileged spiritual status. An embodiment of traditional satire on the gluttonous and self-indulgent Benedictine, he seems to stand at the precise balancing point between preacher and jester, celebrating his success among barons, and claiming that this success is equalled in the spiritual sphere. Yet his poems also function as sermons: they are misogynistic, condemn social folly and praise those who preserve the status quo. These bawdy narratives can be said to function as burlesqued, but conservative, homilies with *exempla*, larded with flattery for a secular patron.

The dialogues may be contrasted with Peire Cardenal's song 'Un sirventes novel vueill comensar' (*PC* 335, 67, XXXVI), in which the speaker imagines a completely different relationship with the divine realm. In this song, the speaker intends to make a powerful plea at the heavenly court, and to strike a deal with God that would reverse the received notion of divine justice: since he did not ask to be born, his sins were not intentional and he should, in his opinion, be returned to the point of his birth (vv. 37–40). The speaker describes the ideal situation he would like to see: the Devil dispossessed (vv. 17–24) and Heaven open to all comers (vv. 25–32). The song ends with a prayer to the Virgin for intercession (vv. 45–8). Peire Cardenal's song reflects a different social and religious milieu to that of the Monk. After 1215, preaching campaigns in the Languedoc aimed to redress what were perceived as flaws in knowledge of doctrine, and to inspire listeners with a combination of awe and fear. Peire's speaker rebels against a vision of God as an exclusively punitive deity, and seems to present a parodic plea for mercy, in which the notion of divine love is stretched to the utmost. There is no hint of the cosy relationship the Monk of Montaudon seems to enjoy with his God a few decades earlier.

Ultimately, the secularization of sacred material is a fraught process, exacerbated by the political and religious tensions of the thirteenth century, but equally difficult to negotiate in the twelfth. Peire Cardenal's defensive *predicator*, who promises his audience a more cheerful song after its patient endurance of his sermon, may play on the same tensions as a televised British comedian, required to play the fool, yet to articulate serious political material. This performed sermonizing will, in principle, keep the audience in the belief that its secular, commercialized and far from radical political views are in some way subversive; it is possible that these preachers wearing the mask of parodists are playing on the same mechanism.

Notes to Chapter 5

1. Stephen Wagg, 'Punching Your Weight: Conversations with Jo Brand', in *Because I Tell A Joke or Two: Comedy, Politics and Social Difference*, ed. Stephen Wagg (London: Routledge, 1998), 111–36 (114–15).
2. Umberto Eco, 'The frames of comic "Freedom"', in *Carnival!*, ed. Thomas H. Sebeok (Berlin: Mouton, 1984), 1–10.
3. See Gaunt, *Troubadours and Irony*, 119–20; see also Dorothy Sutherland, 'L'élément théâtral dans la *canso* chez les troubadours de l'époque classique', *Revue de langue et de littérature d'Oc* 12–13 (1962–3), 95–101; Sarah Kay, *Subjectivity in Troubadour Poetry* (Cambridge: Cambridge University Press, 1990), 130–72.

4. See Harvey, *'Joglars'*, and Miriam Cabré, *'Ne suy joglars, ne.n fay captenemens*: L'ofici de trobador segons Cerverí de Girona', in *Toulouse à la croisée des cultures*, ed. François Pic (Pau: AIEO, 1997), i. 211–24.
5. Cohen, 'Peirol's Vielle'; the text is in de Riquer, *Los Trovadores*, ii. 927.
6. Bartsch, *Chrestomathie provençale*, cols. 231–4.
7. Monson, *Les 'Ensenhamens' occitans*, 153–4.
8. Paul Meyer, 'Notice de quelques manuscrits de la collection Libri à Florence', *Romania* 14 (1885), 485–548.
9. Camille Chabaneau, 'Traduction des psaumes de la pénitence en vers provençaux', *Revue des Langues Romanes* 19 (1881), 209–41; and 'Paraphrase des litanies en vers provençaux', *Revue des Langues Romanes* 29 (1886), 209–55.
10. Camille Chabaneau, 'Paraphrase des psaumes de la pénitence', *Revue des Langues Romanes* 20 (1881), 69–85.
11. Chabaneau, 'Traduction des psaumes', 210 n. 3, 232–3.
12. Chabaneau, 'Paraphrase des litanies', 69–85.
13. See Zorzi, *Valori religiosi*, 73–5.
14. Nelli, *Ecrivains anticonformistes*, ii. 335–55; Pilar Olivella Madrid, 'A propos de l'œuvre de Raimon de Cornet copiée en Catalogne', *Bulletin de l'AIEO* 14 (1998), 51–63 (52).
15. Nelli, *Ecrivains anticonformistes*, ii. 337–9.
16. Olivella Madrid, 'A propos de l'œuvre de Raimon de Cornet', 51 n. 52 and 56 n. 74.
17. See Menache, *Vox Dei*, 78–123 (105).
18. Michel Zink, *La Prédication en langue romane avant 1300* (Paris: Champion, 1982), 440–50, 450 n. 56, from MS Tortosa 106, III, ll. 83–4, ed. A. Thomas, 'Homélies provençales tirées d'un manuscrit de Tortosa', *Annales du Midi* 9 (1897), 369–410 (380).
19. Zink, *La Prédication*, 391–2.
20. Zink, *La Prédication*, 391–9.
21. Zink, *La Prédication*, 222–4.
22. Miriam Cabré, *Cerverí de Girona and his Poetic Traditions* (London: Tamesis, 1999), 78–81.
23. de Riquer, *Cerverí de Girona*, p. ix.
24. Zink, *La Prédication*, 440.
25. *PSW*, i. 266–7; *FEW*, iii. 471–2; Vulgate: 'haereticum hominem post unam et secundam correptionem devita'.
26. My transcription. Paris BN 3548b. See Camille Chabaneau, 'Sermons et préceptes religieux en langue d'Oc du XIIe siècle', *Revue des Langues Romanes* 18 (1880), 105–46; 22 (1882), 157–79; 23 (1883), 53–70, 157–69. See also Hasenohr, 'La prédication aux fidèles'.
27. Sharman, *PC* 242, 1, XVIII, vv. 23–5, 34–6; 242, 72, XXX, vv. 37, 56–9, 78; cf. *PC* 242, 33, LI, vv. 23–33; 242, 54, LXVII, vv. 45–8, 51; 242, 73, LXXV, vv. 110–12.
28. C. A. Robson, *Maurice de Sully and the Medieval Vernacular Homily* (Oxford: Clarendon Press, 1952); Phyllis Barzillay Roberts, *'Stephanus de Lingua-Tonante': Studies in the Sermons of Stephen Langton* (Toronto: PIMS, 1968), 47.
29. Michael Routledge, *Les Poésies du Moine de Montaudon* (Montpellier: Presses de l'Université Paul Valéry, 1977), 13–15.
30. J. Grier, 'A New Voice in the Monastery', 1024.

31. Routledge, *Les Poésies du Moine de Montaudon*, 122–3.
32. Brian J. Levy, *The Comic Text: Patterns and Images in the Old French Fabliaux* (Amsterdam and Atlanta: Rodopi, 2000), 162–7.
33. Zink, *La Prédication*, 373, citing Mazarine 788, f. 130.

CONCLUSION

Peire Cardenal's *sirventes* 'Bel m'es qui bastis' (*PC* 335, 10, Lavaud, XLV) is a text which presents an attack on noblemen who abuse their position and acquire nothing by way of salvation or profit from their sins. The opening, however, is a statement about the creation of a chain of texts through passing on a single unit down a line of performers:

> Bel m'es qui bastis
> Sirventes faitis
>   De faisson.
> Bel e ses totz sis,
> D'amor gent assis
>   En gai son.
> Pueis cals que l'aprenda,
> Abanz que.l reprenda,
>   Regart la razon
> Pueis lo don o.l venda
> A tal que.l revenda
> Can veira sazon
>   E.l retraia
>   Lai don aia
> Anel o cordon,
>   O assaia
>   So de saia:
> Rauba de Gordon.
> (vv. 1–18)

[I like anyone who builds an elegant *sirventes* in his own style, handsome and uncompromising, based attractively upon love, to a cheerful melody. For then whoever takes it up, before learning it, will look at its argument [*razo*]; then he will give it or sell it to someone who will sell it on when he sees the time come, and perform it in a place where he'll receive a ring or a necklace, or will try this on as a tunic: a gown from Gourdon.]

The poet composes an elegant and idiosyncratic product, which will be picked up by a discerning purchaser, who will examine its *razon*, its argument, on top of the aesthetic appeal of the song. The purchaser is only the first in a series of later customers for this song, however: the next one along, who buys it from him, is set to continue this line of transmission, in the hope of acquiring remuneration from performances. This opening would seem to confirm William Burgwinkle's thesis in *Love for Sale* that the troubadour lyric was transmitted and thrived through its cultivation of the nascent capitalism of the Mediterranean basin in the later twelfth to thirteenth centuries. Peire points out that the third or fourth performer down the line may receive the greatest reward from the song, but also notes that the *sirventes* itself is 'de faisson' (v. 3): it is inseparable from its author.

This attitude towards song production is explained by the *vida* of Peire Cardenal, signed by Miquel de la Tor, who claims that Cardenal employed *joglars* to perform his songs. As author, Peire would be present at the performance and would explain the *razo* of the piece, thereby endorsing and signing it, while the *joglar* sang it, and was, presumably, rewarded for his skill (*BS*, L). This opening may, therefore, be read as an advertisement by Peire Cardenal, the author, to potential performers. His songs, if used in the correct transactional mode, will bring great material rewards to those to whom they are sold. It also emphasizes the need to keep the song in circulation. It cannot be left to stagnate, but must be sold on at the right time. However, the rest of Peire's song appears to envisage the pursuit of material profit in quite a different light, since it is wholly concerned with the barren rewards of corrupt behaviour.

This song may be another example of the move noted in 'Predicator' towards making spiritual moralizing more pragmatically and socially oriented, but it also suggests a further conclusion. Peire's introduction into this text of a vision of troubadour songs as elements to be kept eternally in circulation, sold from one singer to the next, but without any loss of the original author's intention, may set the seal on the motivating force behind the chain of parodies, counter-parodies and related rewritings that I have examined so far. The *versus tripertitus caudatus* is maintained and never fully lost throughout the series of reappropriations it endures. It is rewritten, enlarged, fragmented, alternately broken and recuperated; it carries denunciations of sexual excess, presents the possibility of ascetic withdrawal, and attempts to teach, humiliate and entertain. At one level, it is invariably the vehicle of *castiar*. On another, it is open to all varieties of interpretation. Somewhere along the line, every troubadour in this chain, from *c.*1110 to *c.*1275, is aware of the work of Guilhem IX and of the hypotext behind his, and their, rewriting; these songs function as palimpsests. There is a case for saying that the parodies I have examined never lose sight of their sacred model, and appear to struggle both to break from it, and to return towards it.

The reward of the poet or the comedian is invariably envisaged as the gift received for performance. The social role of such a performer is as impossible to assess in its entirety as that of a single parodic text; the culture which produces parodies and comedies is as diverse as the number of individuals comprising its audiences. The responsibility for perpetuating any text, parodic dialogue or performance rests in the hand of its performers and transmitters, but the burden of interpretation is on the audience.

It is also worth noting that the 'rauba de Gordon' may be a tunic, but may equally well signify booty; the customs of the town of Gourdon specifically forbade its inhabitants to buy stolen goods: 'Conduma es de Gordo que nulhs hom [...] de Gordo sabens no compre rauba ni prea ni cauza panada en esta vila ni deforas' [It is a custom of Gourdon that no man of Gourdon may knowingly buy booty, loot nor anything stolen in this town or outside it] (*PSW*, vii. 43–4). If Peire's *sirventes* is using a form taken from a previous poem (as is the case), he is complicit in the selling of stolen goods to a knowing buyer. In other words, the act of performing a text rewritten with critical difference may, according to the interpretation placed upon it, indicate a gift or a knowing theft in the hands of a performer two, three or four versions down the line. It may be a recuperation or a travesty of the original by an individual who may come to share in the debasement wrought on the model. The chain of parodies may end either with the sermon 'Predicator', or with the *estribot*; both songs by Peire Cardenal are the work of a former canon indulging in *prozels trasgitatz*.

Ultimately, the troubadour who chooses either to preach or to sing an entertaining song is involved in the process of drawing on a common stock of materials, texts and melodies, in order to ensure that his words may please his audience. In examining the roles of doctrine and sacred singing, as well as those of scribal practice and recollection techniques, this study has only addressed a small number of the many issues surrounding the composition and performance of such chains of texts. The field of *fin'amors* and its attendant courtly anxieties has not been explored; nor has political satire or moralizing poetry. The main performer under scrutiny has been the clerk, especially the former canon, and his ambiguous relationship with the secular world that he inhabited as a poet who was also a *joglar*, alluding to a common fund of sacred and not so sacred texts. Whether transgressive or recuperative, the parodic texts have displayed a common concern with forms of knowledge and with the aspects of formal and content-based recognition that are inherent in any game played between initiates. The ensuing dialogues show the extent to which a chain of borrowing can reveal parodic strategies at their most exacerbated, as well as at their most extensive.

BIBLIOGRAPHY

Primary Sources

ADAM DE SAINT-VICTOR:

Les Proses d'Adam de Saint-Victor: Textes et musique, précédées d'une étude critique, ed. E. Misset and Pierre Aubry (Paris: Welter, 1900).

The Liturgical Poetry of Adam de Saint-Victor (from the text by Gautier), ed. Digby S. Wrangham, 3 vols. (London: Kegan Paul Trench, 1881).

BERNART MARTI:

Il Trovatore Bernart Marti, ed. Fabrizio Beggiato (Modena: Mucchi, 1984).

BERNART DE VENTADORN:

Bernard de Ventadour: Seine Lieder, ed. Carl Appel (Halle: Niemeyer, 1915).

Carmina Burana, ed. Alfons Hilka and Otto Schumann, 3 vols. (Heidelberg: Winter, 1930–70).

CERVERÍ DE GIRONA:

Obras Completas del trovador Cerverí de Girona: Texto, traducción y notas, ed. Martín de Riquer (Barcelona: Instituto Español de Estudios Mediterráneos, 1947).

Disticha Catonis: Elie's de Wincestre, eines Anonymus, und Everarts Übertragungen des Disticha Catonis, ed. Edmund Max Stengel (Ausgaben und Abhandlungen aus dem Gebiete der romanischen Philologie, 47; Marburg: Elwert, 1886).

GARIN D'APCHIER:

I Sirventesi di Garin d'Apchier e di Torcafol, ed. Fortunata Latella (Modena: Mucchi, 1994).

GIRAUT DE BORNELH:

The 'Cansos' and 'Sirventes' of the Troubadour Giraut de Borneil, ed. Ruth Verity Sharman (Cambridge: Cambridge University Press, 1989).

GUILHEM IX:

Guglielmo IX d'Aquitania, ed. Nicolò Pasero (Modena: Mucchi, 1979).

GUILLEM DE BERGUEDÁ:

Guillem de Berguedá, ed. Martín de Riquer, 2 vols. (Poblet: Abadía de Poblet, 1971).

GUILLEM DE TUDELA (and ANON.):

La Chanson de la Croisade Albigeoise, ed. Eugène Martin-Chabot, trans. Henri Gougaud (Paris: Librairie Générale Française, 1989).

GUIRAUT RIQUIER:
Die Werke der Troubadours, in provenzalischer Sprache, ed. C. A. F. Mahn, 4 vols. (Berlin: Duemmlers, 1853), IV, ed. S. L. H. Pfaff.
LANFRANC CIGALA:
Il Canzionere di Lanfranc Cigala, ed. Francesco Branciforti (Florence: Olschki, 1954).
MARCABRU:
Les Poésies du troubadour Marcabru, ed. J. M. L. Dejeanne (Toulouse: Privat, 1909).
MONK OF MONTAUDON:
Les Poésies du Moine de Montaudon, ed. Michael J. Routledge (Montpellier: Presses de l'Université Paul Valéry, 1977)
PEIRE D'ALVERNHA:
Die Lieder Peire von Auvergne, ed. Rudolf Zenker (Erlangen: Junge, 1900).
Peire d'Alvernha: Liriche, ed. Alberto Del Monte (Turin: Loescher-Cantore, 1955).
PEIRE CARDENAL:
Poésies complètes du troubadour Peire Cardenal, ed. René Lavaud (Toulouse: Privat, 1957).
PEIRE DE COURBIAN:
ALFRED JEANROY and GIULIO BERTONI (eds.), 'Le *Thezaur* de Peire de Courbian', *Annales du Midi* 23 (1921), 290–400.
RAIMON DE CASTELNOU:
Raimon de Castelnou: Canzoni e dottrinale, ed. Andrea Giannetti (Bari: Adriatica, 1988).
Le Sponsus: Mystère des Vierges sages et des Vierges folles, ed. Lucien-Paul Thomas (Paris: Presses universitaires de France, 1951)
WALTER OF CHÂTILLON:
Moralisch-satirische Gedichte Walters von Châtillon, ed. Karl Strecker (Heidelberg: Winter, 1929).

Secondary Sources

ADAM, PAUL, *La Vie paroissiale en France au XIVe siècle* (Paris: Sirey, 1964).
AURELL, MARTIN, *La Vielle et l'épée: troubadours et politique en Provence au XIIIe siècle* (Paris: Aubier, 1989).
AVALLE, D'Arco Silvio, *La letteratura medievale in lingua d'Oc nella sua tradizione manoscritta. Problemi de critica testuale* (Turin: Einaudi, 1961).
BABCOCK, BARBARA A., *The Reversible World: Symbolic Inversion in Art and Society* (Ithaca: Cornell University Press, 1978).
BAKHTIN, MIKHAIL M., *Rabelais and his World*, trans. Hélène Iswolsky (Bloomington: Indiana University Press, 1984).
BARDELL, MATTHEW, 'The allegorical landscape: Peire Vidal's "ric thesaur"',

unpublished paper presented at a postgraduate conference on 'Memory', University of Bristol Centre for Medieval Studies, Bristol, April 1998.

BARTHOLOMAEIS, V. DE, 'Avanzi di un canzionere provenzale del secolo XIII', *Studi Romanzi* 12 (1915), 139–86.

BARTSCH, KARL, *Denkmäler des provenzalischen Litteratur*, reprint of 1856 edn. (Amsterdam: Rodopi, 1966).

—— *Chrestomathie provençale (X^e–XVe siècles)*, 6th edn, reworked by Eduard Koschwitz (Marburg: Elwert, 1904)

BAYLESS, MARTHA, *Parody in the Middle Ages: The Latin Tradition* (Ann Arbor: University of Michigan Press, 1996).

BEC, PIERRE, *Burlesque et obscénité chez les troubadours: Pour une approche du contre-texte médiéval* (Paris: Stock, 1984).

—— *Vièles ou violes?: Variations philologiques et musicales autour des instruments à archet du Moyen Age (XIe–XVe siècle)* (Paris: Klincksieck, 1992).

BECK, JEAN, *La Musique des troubadours* (Paris: Stock, 1979).

BELTRAN, VINCENÇ, 'Tipos y temas trovadorescos. XIV. Alfonso X, Raimon de Castelnou y la corte literaria de Rodez', in *Le Rayonnement des troubadours: Actes du Colloque de l'AIEO, Association Internationale d'Etudes Occitanes, Amsterdam, 16–18 octobre 1995*, ed. Anton Touber (Amsterdam and Atlanta: Rodopi, 1998), 19–39.

BERTONI, GIULIO (ed.), *Il canzionere provenzale di Bernart Amoros (Complemento Càmpori)* (Fribourg: Gschwend, 1911).

BURGWINKLE, WILLIAM E., *Love For Sale: Materialist Readings of the Troubadour Razo Corpus* (New York: Garland, 1997).

BYNUM, CAROLINE WALKER, *Jesus as Mother: Studies in the Spirituality of the High Middle Ages* (Berkeley: University of California Press, 1982).

CABRÉ, MIRIAM, *Cerverí de Girona and his Poetic Traditions* (London: Tamesis, 1999).

—— '*Ne suy joglars, ne.n fay capteniments*: l'ofici de trobador segons Cerverí de Girona', in *Toulouse à la croisée des cultures: Actes du Ve Congrès international de l'Association Internationale d'Etudes Occitanes, Toulouse, 19–24 août 1996*, ed. François Pic, 2 vols. (Pau: AIEO, 1997), i. 211–24.

CAMILLE, MICHAEL, *Image on the Edge: The Margins of Medieval Art* (London: Reaktion Books, 1992).

—— *The Medieval Art of Love: Objects and Subjects of Desire* (London: Laurence King, 1998).

CARERI, MARIA, *Il Canzionere provenzale H (Vat. lat. 3207); Struttura, contenuto e fonti* (Modena: Mucchi, 1990).

CARRUTHERS, MARY, *The Book of Memory: A Study of Memory in Medieval Culture* (Cambridge: Cambridge University Press, 1990).

CHABANEAU, CAMILLE, 'Traduction des psaumes de la pénitence en vers provençaux', *Revue des Langues Romanes* 19 (1881), 209–41.

—— 'Sermons et préceptes religieux en langue d'Oc du XIIe siècle', *Revue des Langues Romanes* 18 (1880), 105–46; 22 (1882), 157–79; 23 (1883), 53–70, 157–69.

—— 'Paraphrase des psaumes de la pénitence', *Revue des Langues Romanes* 20 (1881), 69–85.

—— 'Paraphrase des litanies en vers provençaux', *Revue des Langues Romanes* 29 (1886), 209–55.

CHAILLEY, JACQUES, *L'Ecole musicale de Saint-Martial-de-Limoges, jusqu'à la fin du XIe siècle* (Paris: Les livres essentiels, 1960).

—— 'Les premiers troubadours et les *versus* de l'école d'Aquitaine', *Romania* 76 (1955), 212–39.

—— 'Sur la rythmique des proses victoriennes', *Festschrift Karl Gustav Fellerer*, ed. Heinrich Hüschen (Regensburg: G. Bosse, 1962), 77–81.

CHAMBERS, FRANK M., 'Imitation of Form in the Old Provençal Lyric', *Romance Philology* 6 (1952–3), 104–20.

—— '*D'Aisso lau Dieu* and Aldric del Vilar', *Romance Philology* 35 (1981–2), 489–500.

—— *An Introduction to Old Provençal Versification* (Philadelphia: American Philosophical Society, 1985).

CINGOLANI, STEFANO, 'The *sirventes-ensenhamen* of Guerau de Cabrera: A proposal for a new interpretation', *Journal of Hispanic Research* 1 (1992–3), 191–200.

CLANCHY, MICHAEL T., *From Memory to Written Record: England 1066–1307* (London: Edward Arnold, 1979).

COHEN, JOEL, 'Peirol's Vielle: Instrumental Participation in the Troubador Repertory', *Historical Performance* 3/2 (1990), 73–7.

COLEMAN, JANET, *Ancient and Medieval Memories: Studies in the Reconstruction of the Past* (Cambridge: Cambridge University Press, 1992).

CONTINI, GIANFRANCO, 'A propos de *tribu martel*', *Romania* 63 (1937), 253–66.

COSTA, EUGENIO, *Tropes et séquences dans le cadre de la vie liturgique au Moyen Age* (Rome: C.L.V. Edizioni liturgiche, 1979).

DIEHL, PATRICK S., *The Medieval European Religious Lyric: An Ars Poetica* (Berkeley: University of California Press, 1985).

DRONKE, PETER, *The Medieval Lyric* (London: Hutchinson University Library, 1968).

—— *Medieval Latin Poetry and the Rise of European Love Lyric*, 2 vols. (2nd edn. Oxford: Oxford University Press, 1968).

DUVERNOY, JEAN, *Le Registre d'Inquisition de Jacques Fournier (évèque de Pamiers), 1318–1325*, 3 vols. (Paris: Mouton, 1978).

ECO, UMBERTO, 'The Frames of Comic "Freedom"', in *Carnival!*, ed. Thomas H. Sebeok (Berlin: Mouton, 1984), 1–10.

ELFVING, LARS, *Etude lexicographique sur les séquences limousines* (Stockholm: Almqvist & Wiksell, 1962).

EMMERSON, RICHARD K., *Antichrist in the Middle Ages: A Study of Medieval Apocalypticism, Art and Literature* (Seattle: University of Washington Press, 1981).

ERRANTE, GUIDO, *Marcabru e li fonte sacre dell'antica lirica romanza* (Florence: Sansoni, 1948).

EVANS, PAUL, *The Early Trope Repertory of Saint Martial of Limoges* (Princeton: Princeton University Press, 1970).

FASSLER, MARGOT, 'Who was Adam de Saint-Victor? The Evidence of the Sequence Manuscripts', *Journal of the American Musicological Society* 37 (1984), 233–69.

FRATTI, ANIELLO, 'Un probabile caso di adattamento redazionale diacronico: la canzone-sirventese "Be m'es plazen" (*PC* 323, 10) di Peire d'Alvernhe', *Studi Mediolatini e Volgari* 39 (1993), 33–55.

GAUNT, SIMON, *Troubadours and Irony* (Cambridge: Cambridge University Press, 1989).

—— 'Marginal Men, Marcabru and orthodoxy: the early troubadours and adultery', *Medium Aevum* 59 (1990), 55–72.

—— and KAY, SARAH (eds.), *The Troubadours: An Introduction* (Cambridge: Cambridge University Press, 1999).

GENETTE, GÉRARD, *Palimpsestes: La littérature au second degré* (Paris: Seuil, 1982).

GOBIN, PIERRE, 'La susceptibilité du "parodié": Fausses parodies et mystifications idéologiques', in *Dire la Parodie*, ed. Thomson and Pagès, 107–30.

GODDARD, RICHARD, 'The Early Troubadours and the Latin Tradition', D.Phil. thesis, Oxford, 1986.

GOLOPENTIA-ERETESCU, SANDA, 'La parodie et la feinte', in *Dire la Parodie*, ed. Thomson and Pagès, 35–66.

GRAVDAL, KATHRYN, *Vilain et Courtois: Transgressive Parody in French Literature of the Twelfth and Thirteenth Centuries* (Lincoln, NE: University of Nebraska Press, 1989).

GREENBLATT, STEPHEN, 'Filthy Rites', in *Learning to Curse: Essays in Early Modern Culture* (New York and London: Routledge, 1990), 59–79.

GREIMAS, A.-J. (ed.), *Dictionnaire de l'ancien français jusqu'au milieu du XIVe siècle* (Paris: Larousse, 1980).

GRIER, JAMES, 'A New Voice in the Monastery: Tropes and Versus from Eleventh- and Twelfth-Century Aquitaine', *Speculum* 69 (1994), 1023–69.

GRIVEL, CHARLES, 'Le retournement parodique des discours à leurres constants', in *Dire la Parodie*, ed. Thomson and Pagès, 1–34.

GRUBER, JÖRN, *Die Dialektik des Trobar: Untersuchungen zur Struktur und Entwicklung des occitanischen und französischen Minnesangs des 12. Jahrhunderts* (Tübingen: Niemeyer, 1983).

HARVEY, RUTH E., *The Troubadour Marcabru and Love* (London: Westfield College, 1989).

—— 'The satirical use of the courtly expression *sidons* in the works of the troubadour Marcabru', *Modern Language Review* 78 (1983), 24–33.

—— '*Joglars* and the professional status of the early troubadours', *Medium Aevum* 62 (1993), 221–41.

HASENOHR, GENEVIÈVE, 'La prédication aux fidèles dans la première moitié du XIIe siècle: L'enseignement des sermons "limousins"', *Romania* 116 (1998), 34–67.

HAURÉAU, BARTHÉLÉMY, *Notices et extraits de quelques manuscrits latins de la Bibliothèque Nationale*, 6 vols. (Paris: Klincksieck, 1890–93).

HEERS, JACQUES, *Fêtes des fous et carnavals au Moyen Age* (Paris: Seuil, 1978).

HUCHET, JEAN-CHARLES, *Littérature médiévale et psychanalyse: Pour une clinique littéraire* (Paris: Presses Universitaires de France, 1989).

HUGHES, DAVIS, 'Music and meter in liturgical poetry', *Medievalia et Humanistica* 7 (1976), 29–49.

HUTCHEON, LINDA, *A Theory of Parody: The Teachings of Twentieth-Century Art Forms* (London: Methuen, 1985).

JACOBSSON, RITVA, and TREITLER, LEO, 'Tropes and the concept of genre', in *Pax et Sapientia: Studies in Text and Music of Liturgical Tropes and Sequences, in Memory of Gordon Anderson*, ed. Ritva Jacobsson (Stockholm: Almqvist & Wiksell, 1986), 59–89.

JEANROY, ALFRED, *Les Origines de la poésie lyrique en France au moyen âge* (Paris: Champion, 1925).

JENSEN, FREDE, *Provençal Philology and the Poetry of Guillaume de Poitiers* (Odense: Odense University Press, 1983).

KAY, SARAH, *Subjectivity in Troubadour Poetry* (Cambridge: Cambridge University Press, 1990).

KENDRICK, LAURA, *The Game of Love: Troubadour Wordplay* (Berkeley: University of California Press, 1988).

—— 'Jongleur as Propagandist: the ecclesiastical politics of Marcabru's poetry', in *Cultures of Power: Lordship, Status and Process in Twelfth-Century Europe*, ed. Thomas Bisson (Philadelphia: University of Pennsylvania Press, 1995), 259–86.

KRÜLLS-HEPERMANN, CLAUDIA, 'Contextes de transmission médiévaux: manuscrits et notations musicales', in *Contacts de langues, de civilisations et intertextualité: Actes du IIIe Congrès international de l'Association Internationale d'Etudes Occitanes, Montpellier, 20–26 septembre 1990*, ed. Gérard Gouiran, 3 vols. (Montpellier: Centre d'études occitanes de l'Université de Montpellier, 1992), ii. 627–36.

LAFONT, ROBERT, 'Pour rendre à l'oc et aux Normans leur dû: genèse et premier développement de l'art épique gallo-roman', *Cahiers de civilisation médiévale* 42 (1999), 139–78.

LEGGE, MARIA DOMENICA, *Anglo-Norman Literature and its Background* (Oxford: Oxford University Press, 1963).

—— *Anglo-Norman in the Cloisters: The Influence of the Orders upon Anglo-Norman Literature* (Edinburgh: Edinburgh University Press, 1950).

—— 'La versification anglo-normande au XIIe siècle', in *Mélanges offerts à René Crozet*, ed. Pierre Gallais and Jean-Yves Riou, 2 vols. (Poitiers: Centre d'Études Médiévales, 1966), i. 639–43.

LÉGLU, CATHERINE, 'A reading of troubadour insult songs: the *Comunals* cycle', *Reading Medieval Studies* 22 (1996), 63–83.

—— 'Negative self-promotion: the troubadour *sirventes joglaresc*', in *The Court and Cultural Diversity: Selected Papers from the Eighth Triennial Congress of the International Courtly Literature Society, The Queen's University of Belfast, 26 July–1 August 1995*, ed. Evelyn Mullally and John Thompson (Woodbridge and Rochester: D. S. Brewer, 1997), 47–56.

—— 'Defamation in the Troubadour *Sirventes*: Legislation and Lyric Poetry', *Medium Ævum* 66 (1997), 28–41.

LEHMANN, PAUL, *Die Parodie im Mittelalter* (Munich: Drei Masken Verlag, 1922).

LEJEUNE, RITA, 'La forme de l'*ensenhamen au jongleur* du troubadour Guiraut de Cabrera', *Estudis Romànics* 9 (1961), 171–81.

LEVER, MAURICE, *Le Sceptre et la marotte: Histoire des fous de cour* (Paris: Fayard, 1983).

LE VOT, GÉRARD, *Vocabulaire de la musique médiévale* (Paris: Minerve, 1993).

LEVY, BRIAN J., *The Comic Text: Patterns and Images in the Old French Fabliaux* (Amsterdam: Rodopi, 2000).

LINEHAN, PETER, *The Ladies of Zamora* (Manchester: Manchester University Press, 1997).

MADRIGNAC, ANDRÉ and PISTONE, DANIÈLE, *Le Chant Grégorien: historique et pratique* (Paris: Champion, 1981).

MANN, JILL, 'Satiric Subject and Satiric Object in Goliardic Literature', *Mittellateinisches Jahrbuch* 15 (1980), 63–86.

MARSHALL, JOHN, 'Pour l'étude des *contrafacta* dans la poésie des troubadours', *Romania* 101 (1980), 289–335.

MARTINDALE, JANE, '"Cavaleria et Orgueill": Duke William IX of Aquitaine and the Historian', in *The Ideals and Practice of Medieval Knighthood,* II: *Papers from the third Strawberry Hill Conference, 1986,* ed. Christopher Harper-Bill and Ruth Harvey (Woodbridge: Boydell, 1988), 87–116.

MASTERS, BERNADETTE A., *Esthétique et manuscripture: le 'moulin à paroles' au Moyen Age* (Heidelberg: Winter, 1992).

MÉJEAN, SUZANNE, *see* Thiolier-Méjean, Suzanne.

MENACHE, SOPHIA, *The Vox Dei: Communication in the Middle Ages* (Oxford: Oxford University Press, 1990).

MENEGHETTI, MARIA LUISA, 'Un stornello nunziante. Fonti, significato e datazione dei due *vers* dell'estornel di Marcabru', in *'Cantarem d'aquestz trobadors': Studi occitanici in onore di Giuseppe Tavani*, ed. Luciano Rossi (Alessandria: Edizioni dell'Orso, 1995), 47–63.

—— 'Intertextuality and dialogism in the troubadours', in *The Troubadours: An Introduction*, ed. Gaunt and Kay, 181–96.

MEYER, PAUL, 'Anciennes poésies religieuses en langue d'Oc', *Bibliothèque de l'Ecole des Chartes* 5 (1860), 481–97.

—— 'Notice de quelques manuscrits de la collection Libri à Florence', *Romania* 14 (1885), 485–548.

MONSON, DON ALFRED, *Les 'ensenhamens' occitans: essai de définition et de délimitation du genre* (Paris: Klincksieck, 1981).

—— 'The troubadours at play: irony, parody and burlesque', in *The Troubadours: An Introduction*, ed. Gaunt and Kay, 197–211.

MONTEVERDI, A., 'Pier d'Alvergna nel foglio superstite di un canzionere provenzale del duecento', *Studi Medievali* 12 (1939), 133–59.

MUIR, LYNETTE R., *The Biblical Drama of Medieval Europe* (Cambridge: Cambridge University Press, 1995).

MÜLLER, BEATE (ed.), *Parody: Dimensions and Perspectives* (Amsterdam and Atlanta: Rodopi, 1998).

MURRAY, ALEXANDER, *Reason and Society in the Middle Ages* (Oxford: Clarendon Press, 1978).

NELLI, RENÉ, *Ecrivains anti-conformistes du moyen-âge occitan*, II: *Hérétiques et politiques* (Paris: Phébus, 1977).

NOULET, JEAN-BAPTISTE, and CHABANEAU, CAMILLE, *Deux Manuscrits Provençaux du XIVe siècle* (Geneva–Marseille: Slatkine–Laffitte Reprints, 1973).

NYKL, A. R., *Hispano-Arabic Poetry and its Relations with the Old Provençal Troubadours* (Baltimore: J. H. Furst, 1946).

OLIVELLA MADRID, PILAR, 'A propos de l'œuvre de Raimon de Cornet copiée en Catalogne', *Bulletin de l'Association Internationale d'Etudes Occitanes* 14 (1998), 51–63.

OROZ ARISCUREN, FRANCISCO (ed.), *La lírica religiosa en la literatura provenzal antigua: edición crítica, traducción, notas y glosario* (Pamplona: Disputación foral de Navarra, institución Príncipe de Viana, 1972).

PADEN, WILLIAM D., 'The Role of the Joglar in Troubadour Lyric Poetry', in *Chrétien de Troyes and the Troubadours: Essays in Memory of Leslie Topsfield*, ed. Peter S. Noble and Linda M. Paterson (Cambridge: St. Catharine's College, 1984), 90–9.

—— '*De monachis rithmos facientibus*: Hélinant of Froidmont, Bertran de Born and the Cistercian General Chapter of 1199', *Speculum* 55 (1980), 669–85.

PAGE, CHRISTOPHER, *Voice and Instruments of the Middle Ages: Instrumental Practice and Songs in France, 1100–1300* (London: Dent, 1987).

PANUCCIO, CLAUDIA, review of Spaggiari, *Il Nome di Marcabru*, in *Medioevo Romanzo* 19 (1994), 195-200.

PASERO, NICOLÒ, 'Pastora contro cavaliere, Marcabruno contro Guglielmo IX: Fenomeni di intertestualità in "L'autrier jost' una sebissa"', *Cultura Neolatina* 43 (1983), 9–25.

PATERSON, LINDA, *Troubadours and Eloquence* (Oxford: Oxford University Press, 1975).

—— *The World of the Troubadours: Medieval Occitan Society, 1100–1300* (Cambridge: Cambridge University Press, 1993).

PFEFFER, WENDY, *Proverbs in Medieval Occitan Literature* (Gainesville: University of Florida Press, 1997).

PIROT, FRANÇOIS, *Recherches sur les connaissances littéraires des troubadours occitans et catalans des XIIe et XIIIe siècles: les 'sirventes-ensenhamens' de Guerau de Cabrera, Guiraut de Calanson et Bertrand de Paris* (Barcelona: Real Academia de Buenas Letras, 1972).

PODHRASKY, GERHARD, *New Dictionary of Liturgy*, ed. and trans. Lancelot Sheppard (London: Geoffrey Chapman, 1967).

POE, ELIZABETH W., '*Pos podetz sequir las rimas contrasemblantz*: Imitators of the Master Troubadour Giraut de Bornelh', in *The Medieval 'Opus': Imitation, Rewriting, and Transmission in the French Tradition. Proceedings of the Symposium held at the Institute for Research in the Humanities, October 5–7 1995, the University of Wisconsin—Madison*, ed. Douglas Kelly (Amsterdam and Atlanta: Rodopi, 1997), 279–97.

POLLINA, VINCENT, *'Si Cum Marcabrus Declina': Studies in the Poetics of the Troubadour Marcabru* (Modena: STEM Mucchi, 1991).

RICHLIN, AMY, *The Garden of Priapus: Sexuality and Aggression in Roman Humour* (New Haven: Yale University Press, 1983).

RICKETTS, PETER T., 'L'Estribot, forme et fond', in *Mélanges de langue et de littérature occitanes en hommage à Pierre Bec* (Poitiers: Université de Poitiers, CESCM, 1991), 475–83.

RIEGER, DIETMAR, *Gattungen und Gattungsbezeichnungen der Trobadorlyrik* (Tübingen: Niemeyer, 1976).

DE RIQUER, MARTÍN (ed.), *Los Trovadores: historia literaria y textos*, 3 vols. (Barcelona: Planeta, 1975).

ROBERTS, PHYLLIS BARZILLAY, *'Stephanus de lingua-tonante': Studies in the Sermons of Stephen Langton* (Toronto: PIMS, 1968).

ROBSON, C. A., *Maurice de Sully and the Medieval Vernacular Homily* (Oxford: Clarendon Press, 1952).

RONCAGLIA, AURELIO, 'Il *gap* di Marcabruno', *Studi Medievali* 17 (1951), 46–70.

—— 'Riflessi di posizioni cistercensi nella poesia del XII secolo: Discussione sui fondamenti religiosi del 'trobar naturau' di Marcabruno', in *I Cistercensi e il lazio: Atti delle giornate di studio dell'Istituto di Storia dell'Arte dell' Università di Roma, 17–22 maggio 1977* (Rome: Multigrafica, 1978), 11–22.

ROSE, MARGARET A., *Parody: Ancient, Modern and Post-Modern* (Cambridge: Cambridge University Press, 1993).

ROSSI, LUCIANO, 'Per l'interpretazione di "Cantarai d'aquests trobadors" (323, 11)', in *'Cantarem d'aquestz trobadors': Studi occitanici in onore di Giuseppe Tavani*, ed. Luciano Rossi (Alessandria: Edizioni dell'Orso, 1995), 65–111.

ROUSE, RICHARD, M. and ROUSE, MARY A., '*Statim invenire*: Schools, Preachers, and New Attitudes to the Page', in *Authentic Witnesses: Approaches to Medieval Texts and Manuscripts*, ed. Richard M. Rouse and Mary A. Rouse (Notre Dame: University of Notre Dame Press, 1991), 191–219.

SAFFIOTI, TITO, *I Giullari in Italia: Lo spettacolo, il pubblico, i testi* (Milan: Xenia, 1990).

SCHELUDKO, DMITRI, 'Die Marienlieder in der altprovenzalischen Lyrik', *Neuphilologische Mitteilungen* 37 (1936), 15–42.

—— 'Über die religiöse Lyrik der Troubadours', *Neuphilologische Mitteilungen* 38 (1937), 224–50.

SCHUBERT, MARTIN J., 'Parody in Thirteenth-Century German Poetry', in *Parody: Dimensions and Perspectives*, ed. Müller, 237–73.

SMITH, CYRIL E., *The University of Toulouse in the Middle Ages* (Milwaukee: Marquette University Press, 1958).

SPAGGIARI, BARBARA, *Il Nome di Marcabru: Contributi di onomastica e critica testuale* (Spoleto: Centro Italiano di studi sull'alto medioevo, 1992).

—— 'Artimalec e *Archimalec*', *Romania* 111 (1990), 331–45.

SPANKE, HANS, 'St-Martial Studien. Ein Beitrag zur frühromanischen Metrik', *Zeitschrift für französische Sprache und Literatur* 54 (1930–1), 282–317, 385–422.

—— *Beziehungen zwischen Romanischer und Mittellateinischer Lyrik: Mit besonderer Berücksichtigung der Metrik und Musik* (Abhandlungen der Gesellschaft der Wissenschaften zu Göttingen, philologisch-historische Klasse, Dritte Folge, 18; Berlin and Göttingen: Vandenhoek und Ruprecht, 1936).

—— *Untersuchungen über die Ursprünge des romanischen Minnesangs: Marcabrustudien* (Abhandlungen der Gesellschaft der Wissenschaften zu Göttingen, philologisch-historische Klasse, Dritte Folge, 24; Göttingen: Vandenhoek und Ruprecht, 1940).

STÄDTLER, KATHARINA, 'The *Sirventes* of Gormonda de Montpeslier', in *The Voice of the Trobairitz: Perspectives on the Women Troubadours*, ed. William D. Paden (Philadelphia: Pennsylvania University Press, 1989), 129–37.

STEVENS, JOHN, *Words and Music in the Middle Ages: Song, Narrative, Dance and Drama, 1050–1350* (Cambridge: Cambridge University Press, 1986).

STOROST, JOACHIM, *Ursprung und Entwicklung des altprovenzalischen Sirventes bis auf Bertran de Born* (Halle: Niemeyer, 1931).

SUCHIER, HERMANN, *Denkmäler der provenzalischen Literatur und Sprache* (Halle: Niemeyer, 1883).

—— (ed.), *Zwei altfranzösische Reimpredigten*, reworked by Walter Suchier (Halle: Niemeyer, 1949).

SUTHERLAND, DOROTHY R., 'L'élément théâtral dans la *canso* chez les troubadours de l'époque classique', *Revue de langue et de littérature d'Oc* 12–13 (1962–3), 95–101.

SWITTEN, MARGARET, 'Modèle et variations: Saint-Martial-de-Limoges et les troubadours', in *Contacts de langues, de civilisations et intertextualité: Actes du IIIe Congrès international de l'Association Internationale d'Etudes Occitanes, Montpellier, 20–26 septembre 1990*, ed. Gérard Gouiran, 3 vols. (Montpellier: Centre d'Etudes Occitanes de l'Université de Montpellier, 1992), ii. 679–96.

TANQUEREY, F. J. (ed.), *Le Roman des Romans et le Sermon en Vers (Oyez, seignurs, sermun): Deux poèmes moraux anglo-français* (Paris: Champion, 1922).

TAVERA, ANTOINE, 'Le congé de Peire d'Auvergne: un problème d'édition', in *Actes du Ve Congrès international de langue et de littérature d'oc et d'études franco-provençales, Nice, 6–12 septembre 1967*, ed. Gérard Miognet and Roger Lassalle (Paris: Les Belles Lettres, 1974), 444–56.

THIOLIER-MÉJEAN, SUZANNE, *Les Poésies satiriques et morales des troubadours du XIIe à la fin du XIIIe siècle* (Paris: Nizet, 1978).

—— 'Contribution à l'étude du *sirventes joglaresc*', in *Mélanges de philologie romane dédiés à la mémoire de Jean Boutière*, ed. Irénée Cluzel and François Pirot, 2 vols. (Liège: Solédi, 1971), i. 377–95.

—— 'De la rupture comme principe esthétique du *sirventes*', in *Studia Occitania in memoriam Paul Rémy*, ed. Hans-Erich Keller, 2 vols. (Kalamazoo: Medieval Institute Publications, Western Michigan University, 1986), ii. 313–22.

—— *La Poétique des troubadours: trois études sur le sirventés* (Paris: Presses de l'Université de Paris-Sorbonne, 1994).

THOMAS, A., 'Homélies provençales tirées d'un manuscrit de Tortosa', *Annales du Midi* 9 (1897), 369–410.

THOMSON, CLIVE and PAGÈS, ALAIN (eds.), *Dire la Parodie: Colloque de Cerisy* (Bern: Peter Lang, 1989).

TOPSFIELD, LESLIE, *Troubadours and Love* (Cambridge: Cambridge University Press, 1975).

TREITLER, LEO, 'Oral, Written and Literate Process in the Transmission of Medieval Music', *Speculum* 56 (1981), 471–91.

VAN DER WERF, HENDRIK, with BOND, GERALD R., *Extant Troubadour Melodies: Transcriptions and Essays for Performers and Scholars* (Rochester, NY: The Author, 1984).

VAN DEUSEN, NANCY, 'Polymelodic sequences and a "second epoch" of sequence composition', *Musicologie Médiévale: Notations et Séquences*, ed. Michel Huglo (Paris: Champion, 1987), 213–25.

VAN VLECK, AMELIA, *Memory and Recreation in the Troubadour Lyric* (Berkeley: University of California Press, 1991).

VATTERONI, SERGIO, 'Peire Cardenal e l'*estribot* nella poesia provenzale', *Medioevo Romanzo* 15 (1990), 61–91.

WAGG, STEPHEN, 'Punching Your Weight: Conversations with Jo Brand', in *Because I Tell a Joke or Two: Comedy, Politics and Social Difference*, ed. Stephen Wagg (London: Routledge, 1998), 111–36.

WAKEFIELD, WALTER L., *Heresy, Crusade and Inquisition in Southern France, 1100–1250* (London: Allen and Unwin, 1974).

WALRAVENS, CHRISTELLE, 'Insultes, blasphèmes ou hérésie? Un procès à l'officialité épiscopale de Troyes en 1445', *Bibliothèque de l'Ecole des Chartes* 154 (1996), 485–507.

WARNER, MARINA, *Alone of all her Sex: The Myth and Cult of the Virgin Mary* (London: Picador, 1983).

WITTHOEFT, FRIEDRICH (ed.), *Sirventes Joglaresc: Ein Blick auf das altfranzösische Spielmannsleben* (Ausgaben und Abhandlungen aus dem Gebiete der romanischen Philologie, vol. 88; Marburg: Elwert, 1891).

YOUNG, KARL, *The Drama of the Medieval Church*, 2 vols. (Oxford: Clarendon Press, 1933).

ZINK, MICHEL, *La Prédication en langue romane avant 1300* (Paris: Champion, 1982).

ZORZI, DIEGO, *Valori religiosi nella letteratura provenzale: la spiritualità trinitaria* (Milan: Società editrice "Vita e Pensiero", 1954).

ZUFFEREY, FRANÇOIS, *Recherches linguistiques sur les chansonniers provençaux* (Geneva: Droz, 1987).

INDEX